Making Sense Out of Sex:
A New Look at Being a Man

Making Sense Out of Sex:

A New Look at Being a Man

Dr. Stephen T. Whelan
and
Dr. Elizabeth M. Whelan

McGRAW-HILL BOOK COMPANY
New York   St. Louis   San Francisco   Auckland   Düsseldorf
Johannesburg   Kuala Lumpur   London   Mexico
Montreal   New Delhi   Panama   Paris   São Paulo   Singapore
Sydney   Tokyo   Toronto

FOR
MICHAEL

Acknowledgments

We would like to thank those people who were particularly helpful to us in the preparation of this book.

Marilyn Bartle typed the numerous versions of this manuscript and, as the mother of a son and two daughters, offered many perceptive comments and insights. Alfred, Michael and Stephen Whelan, Barry Bartle, and Nancy Chapman were among those who critically reviewed the first drafts and added comments that led to improved clarity and preciseness.

Dr. Rodrigo Guerrero, Dean of the University of Valle's (Cali, Colombia) Health Division, Reverend Edward Konopka of Vernon, Connecticut, and Dr. Paul Fitzgerald of Lynchburg, Virginia, generously offered their services as professional evaluators.

We are also indebted to the library staff of the New York Academy of Medicine and the Cornell Medical College for their assistance in locating the vast amount of research material that was necessary in the development of this book.

Library of Congress Cataloging in Publication Data
Whelan, Stephen.
  Making sense out of sex.
  Bibliography: p.
  Includes index.
  SUMMARY: Discusses the physical and social aspects of sex for boys including anatomy, contraceptives, reproduction, sexual relationships, and marriage.
  1. Sex instruction for boys. [1. Sex instruction for boys] I. Whelan, Elizabeth M., joint author. II. Title
HQ41.W47   613.9'53   74-31421
ISBN 0-07-069527-X   0-07-069528-8 lib. bdg.

1234567 BPBP 9898765

Contents

ACKNOWLEDGMENTS   iv

PREFACE   vii

WHY WE WROTE THIS BOOK   xi

Chapter 1
      ONE HUNDRED PERCENT
      MALE—THAT'S YOU   1

Chapter 2
      THE PATH TO MANHOOD . .   13

Chapter 3
      WHEN A GIRL GROWS UP . .   25

Chapter 4
      WHEN THE SPERM AND THE
      EGG BECOME ONE   41

Chapter 5
      BEYOND CONCEPTION   57

Chapter 6
      BIRTH CONTROL: PAST,
      PRESENT, AND FUTURE   71

Chapter 7
        A NEW LOOK AT
        "SEXUAL FREEDOM"   101
Chapter 8
        THE DON JUAN MYTHS   121
Chapter 9
        WHERE ARE YOU
        GOING IN LIFE?   139
WORDS YOU'LL WANT TO KNOW . . .   151
REFERENCES AND
SUGGESTIONS FOR
FURTHER READING   167
INDEX   175

Preface

I have read this book as a psychoanalyst who observes the suffering and treats the damaging effects of serious sexual problems, and have come to the conclusion that *Making Sense Out of Sex* is a most useful and timely volume.

Not so long ago, sex was looked down on as a necessary evil, something to be checked and held in contempt and indulged in only rarely, when necessary for human reproduction. Today, this attitude is old hat and the pendulum has swung far over to the other side. Champions of the so-called sexual revolution consider sex a life force and a fountain of supreme happiness. Instant gratification of sexual desires and sexual pleasure is the goal. In their view love, affection and tenderness, friendship, devotion, commitment and compassion are not necessarily relevant. Widespread common practices of group sex, wife-swapping, swinging, hit-and-run sexual episodes are all expressions of a dehumanized kind of sexuality. No wonder some teenagers—perhaps you among them—feel confused and lost, lacking as they do useful guidelines for sexual conduct.

Poet Archibald MacLeish has this to say about the subject:

> In a healthy, natural society . . . what we call "sex" was the healthy and rational consequence of love. With us it's the other way around. We start with our interest with sex and assume that what then happens is going to be love. It could be, I suppose, but the chances are against it. A couple of eighteen-year-olds—boy and girl—going to bed to exercise themselves sexually aren't going to end up with anything Catullus or Sappho . . . would recognize as love. Which is their loss. But if we follow that habit in our paperbacks and our blue motion pictures, the end results may well be that the corrupted word will corrupt the thing itself. And that would be a loss to all of us—to our humanity—to the meanings of our human lives.

The merit of *Making Sense Out of Sex*, it seems to me, lies not only in providing the reader with the "basic facts about the male and female reproductive systems and the process of conception, pregnancy and birth" and "how various means of contraception prevent pregnancies and allow married couples to postpone or avoid having babies," but above all in placing such valuable information within an emotional, psychological and ethical framework that is so necessary for making intelligent and responsible decisions.

Furthermore, like MacLeish, the authors underline the importance of love, of mutual affection and tenderness, of equality and mutual respect between men and women. In other words, the sexual drive is imbued with human quality. At the same time, of course, we have to keep in mind that the sexual drive and the capacity to love are separate forces acting on each other in a reciprocal way. Love humanizes the sex drive, and the sex drive gives passion and excitement to love.

Considering the heavy concentration on sexual matters starting with the early teen years, you might think the sex drive is absolutely essential for personal survival. Not so. On a scale of priorities, sex is low man on the totem pole of man's vital needs. It comes after breathing, eating, sleeping, the need for protection from the elements, the need to enjoy personal relationships, the need for love, security, and self-esteem.

When all is said and done sex is no more than a desire—true, a powerful desire—and when gratified, one that enriches life immensely. The sexual drive colors the life of the teenager with a palette of excitement. Yet it also frequently leads to feelings of anguish because of the unfortunate gap between sexual coming-of-age at puberty and social maturation about five or ten years later. As a result of this gap, sexual desire in the past was frequently unfulfilled and only found expression in daydreams. Nowadays, the pill, the I.U.D. and other means of contraception have changed the picture. The teenager of today has far more sexual freedom before marriage. In fact, many young people believe it is unnatural for them not to have sexual intercourse during adolescence.

Nevertheless, a promising note has been sounded. A recent survey of adolescents indicates that many young people are against depersonalized and dehumanized sex. Robert C. Sorensen reports in *Adolescent Sexuality in Contemporary America* some noteworthy findings:

–A majority of adolescents oppose having sex for physical pleasure alone.

–Ninety percent of all adolescents believe it is important that they develop their own personal values.

–Three-fourths of all adolescents believe they have not personally participated in sex acts that they would consider immoral or abnormal.

–A love that emphasizes mutuality is considered to be an excellent assurance of sexual satisfaction.

–Love is seen as participation in a self-fulfilling relationship. It embraces both parties, while each maintains his and her own individuality.

–The majority of adolescents . . . guard against using a person or being used sexually.

–The large majority of adolescents intend to marry and have children. But they intend to love and be loved several times before they marry.

These encouraging findings show that for the most part young people are approaching sexual matters with good sense and they are likely to read *Making Sense Out of Sex* with open minds.

Adolescence itself is a vital period in your life. It is your link between childhood and adulthood. Just as the weakest link in a chain determines its strength, so the quality of adolescent experiences determines the strength of you as a person. You will be developing the attributes you have been acquiring all through your childhood—basic trust, independence, initiative and industry. By integrating these into your personality, you gradually achieve a sense of identity. You become a mature, responsible adult. I think *Making Sense Out of Sex* can help you make this all-important transition from childhood to adulthood. It will give you the facts you need for intelligent decision making. Then, it's up to you.

Henry Greenbaum, M.D.
Clinical Associate Professor, Psychiatry
New York University School of Medicine

Why We Wrote This Book

We wrote this book because we feel that young men should know about sex—both about the physical *and* emotional aspects of sex.

When we started this project, we very well understood what Mark Twain meant when he said, "Adam had the best of it. When he said something, he knew no one had ever said it before." There *are* many sex education books for teenagers, but we were going to at least *try* to say something different. There were two reasons we felt there was a need for a book called *Making Sense Out of Sex*.

First, we know (and you probably do by now, too) that the teenage years can be pretty confusing at times. One day people tell you that you've become a man—then the next day they treat you like a little boy again. And the next day they tell you again to "act like a man." You also probably fluctuate in your own image of yourself—that's because you are in a period of transition and things aren't quite as predictable as they once were. In our society there is no real line that marks the transition from childhood to adulthood, although in other cultures there are such lines. For instance, many primitive tribes had what were known as rites of passage in which adolescent girls and boys participated in a type of ceremonial event and emerged as an adult. Then there was no going back, but that is not the case here. Growing up in modern society means going through a prolonged—and sometimes tumultuous—period of years.

Second, we felt there was a need for *Making Sense Out of Sex*, because not only are you going through the normal confusion of young adulthood, but also things are further complicated today by an apparent lack of rules and regulations about sex and other aspects of our lives. For instance, you've probably heard about the so-called sexual revolution. We've come a long way in understanding sexuality and the role it plays in our lives. But in the course of this shift of attitudes, some people have become perplexed about what is and what is not acceptable behavior (someone once described the sexual revolution as "opening all the windows, but forgetting to put the screens on"). And as a result, teenagers have more questions than ever before about the what, when, and with whom of sex.

Before we began writing this book, we asked a number of teenage boys, "What is it that you would like to know about sex?" Most of them emphatically responded, "Everything!" But the everything of sex would consume ten volumes at least. This was a problem, since this book had to be a reasonable length. So we pursued the matter and asked them if they could be more specific about the sex questions that were on their minds. And when we analyzed the issues raised, they appeared to fall into two general categories.

First, these young adults wanted "the facts of life." They were very aware that their bodies were changing dramatically. And they noticed that the young women around them were looking and acting very differently than they were just a couple of years ago. Most of them had heard and read about "where babies come from" and had seen many newspaper and magazine articles about The Pill and other means of avoiding births. But they wanted more details on these fascinating subjects. Second, these teenagers wanted to go beyond the biology books. They wanted to know what role sex was going to play in their lives. They wanted information that would help them make decisions about masturbation, "necking," "petting," and sexual intercourse. They were confused about all the sexual revolution talk they heard and wanted some basic facts that would let them make their own well-informed decisions. Their reaction to the turmoil in today's sexual codes reminded us of a song that Cole Porter wrote a few decades ago. It is called "Anything Goes." Things are changing, but, with all due respect to Cole Porter, anything does not go. And that's one of the topics we'll discuss in detail in *Making Sense Out of Sex*. But first we'll turn our attention to those "facts of life."

In the first six chapters you will read about your own complex reproductive system and how you have developed the capacity to produce male sex cells, or sperm, which can join the female sex cell, or egg, to create a new human life. You'll get the facts about what is happening inside a young woman's body—and about how her reproductive system may sometimes function in a manner that will allow her to nourish, protect, and carry a developing baby. After you have these basic facts about the male and female reproductive systems and the processes of conception, pregnancy, and birth, you'll be able to understand how various means of contraception prevent pregnancies and allow married couples to postpone or avoid having babies.

In the second part of this book, we'll turn from the biology to the psychology of sex. During your teenage years, you may very well be faced with decisions about sexual behavior—and you need some straightforward factual information that will ensure that those decisions are well-informed, responsible ones. Chapters 7, 8, and 9 will give you that information (and will explode some of the common myths about men and sex that have developed over the years). Additionally, these discussions will attempt to start you thinking about your career plans, marriage, and having children, and where these events fit in terms of your life priorities.

You might gather from this brief overview of *Making Sense Out of Sex* that it covers a great deal of territory. Well, it does! As you begin reading it, you will immediately realize that it is not a typical "birds and bees" discussion. We felt that you would not want a superficial discussion of these important and very personal topics. So we will be dealing with some sophisticated—and very complex—issues. You'll have to read this book slowly and carefully if you want to get as much out of it as you can. And you'll probably want to reread certain sections a year or so from now, when the topics may have more relevance to the events occurring in your life. You should think of *Making Sense Out of Sex* as a resource book to which you will want to refer throughout your teenage years.

As you read this book, you should keep in mind that you are

being given more information about human reproduction and sexuality than any other generation of young men. Until recently, there was a prevailing belief that if a young man knew "too much" he would "get into trouble." So teenagers would have to read confusing, vaguely worded descriptions of sexual topics and they would inevitably conclude that sex and reproduction were more mysterious than they had originally thought.

But today it is clear—both to us and to most parents of teenagers—that it is the young men and women who do *not* have the facts who "get into trouble." Those with an awareness of how their body works, and an understanding of the rewards that go with a mature approach to human sexuality, cannot help but develop a deep respect for the impressive potentials they have. And, as a result, they make intelligent, responsible decisions.

It is because of these convictions—and the belief that the facts will help you, not mislead you—that we have prepared the candid, detailed discussion you will find in each of the chapters of *Making Sense Out of Sex*.

You'll be making many important decisions before you reach age twenty. Decisions about sex may be just one of them. But because the wrong decision about sex can have such serious and long-term effects on your life options and activities, it is particularly important that you have the facts. And that's why we wrote this book.

Stephen T. Whelan, M.D.
Merion, Pennsylvania

Elizabeth M. Whelan, Sc.D., M.P.H.
New York, New York

February, 1975

chapter 1

One Hundred Percent Male—That's You

XY = MALE

You have always been aware of your maleness since as far back as you can remember. But recently you have probably been even *more* aware of it than before. And you have more questions than ever before about your reproductive organs and how they function.

Some of those changes that were part of the transition from boyhood to manhood are particularly obvious to you: the increase in size of your sex organs, the hair that is growing in various parts of your body, your spurt in growth, just to mention a few. But those external changes that are most obvious occurred only because of some complex processes that have been at work *inside* your body for a few years now.

There are a number of different ways we could approach the study of your reproductive system and how it works. But because the subject matter is so complex, we have decided to divide it into two different chapters.

In this first chapter, you will get an overview of your inside and outside reproductive parts. You will learn where they are located, what they look like, and generally what they do. You will read about the male reproductive cells, the *sperm*, what they look like and how they are made, and you will become familiar with the parts of your "internal anatomic highway" on which the sperm travel to the outside of your body. Some of these organs and activities may be very familiar to you, but others, especially those that exist and function inside your body, may be less familiar.

As you go through these first few pages, you will find that many of your current questions are still unanswered—and indeed, that additional ones have occurred to you. But consider this first chapter as only an introduction to the male reproductive system. It will be in Chapter 2 that we will turn our attention to *how* sperm are made, and how and when they are released from a man's body.

In presenting the story of what makes a man a male, let's start where any good story does—at the beginning. When do you think your career as a male began? The day you were born? Sometime during the middle or late part of the period when you were developing inside your mother?

IT'S A BOY!

Actually, neither of those answers is correct. You were destined to be a male the very moment your father's sperm cell joined with your mother's egg cell, that is, at the very instant you came into existence.

It was your father's sperm cell that determined which sex you were going to be. He contributed millions of sperm cells to your mother—but only one of them was going to join up with her egg cell to form you. There were two different types of cells competing for the opportunity to create a new life. One type of sperm carried an X, or female-producing chromosome. The other carried a Y, or male-producing sex chromosome. In your case the one successful sperm was the Y variety. And right away, one very important matter was determined: You were going to enter the world as a boy.

Once the determination was made, you immediately began to grow in a manner that, when you were born, would let the world know that you were male. Even before your birth, an elaborate reproductive structure had developed.

TESTES: THE MALE SEX GLANDS

Very early in your prenatal life—that is, in the months before you were born—your *testes*, or *testicles* (the singular is *testis*) began to develop. The testes are the two oval bodies often referred to as the male reproductive or sex glands. You know that both of your testes are now outside your body—in that fleshy pouch known as the scrotum. But these sex glands were not *always* outside your body; they started out *inside* you, growing in your abdomen, the area around your stomach and hipbones. Gradually, however, they did move downward and passed through a special tunnel known as the *inguinal canal*. When they descended into the scrotum, this canal naturally closed up to prevent other tissues from coming out.

The passage of the testes into the scrotum from inside the body usually occurs without any problems, and the whole process is complete by about the eighth or ninth month of pregnancy. When male babies are born, about 96 percent of them have already completed this "testes relocation process." And fully half of the remaining 4 percent do so shortly after their birth. Only rarely do the testes fail to complete their journey through the inguinal canal. If this rare condition does occur, medical help is necessary to put the sex glands in proper position. Otherwise they would be unable to function properly later in life.

There is another related problem you may have heard about. Once in a while, the canal through which the testes pass does not close as tightly as it should—or, because of some type of a strain, it is reopened. This condition (a special type of *hernia*), can usually be corrected by means of simple surgical procedures.

Each of your testes is one-to-two inches long and is shaped something like a plum. You should know that there is a wide variation in the size of testes from man to man—and the size of these glands has nothing whatsoever to do with their ability to function. Similarly, you should be aware that one testicle may hang lower than the other, generally because in humans one of the testes usually is larger than the other.

Inside each testis is a large mass of tiny tubes. It's been estimated that there is well over one mile of tubing in each gland, each tube being so small that it is scarcely thicker than a human hair. But in the cells of these tiny tubes, two important processes take place: the production of sperm, the male sex cells, and the production and secretion of male sex hormones. (You'll read more about these events in the next chapter.)

SCROTUM

As you already know, the testes lie within the *scrotum*, the pouch of loose skin which is divided into two parts, one for each of the male sex glands. Early scientists studying male reproductive parts thought that the scrotum acted as a type of "heavyweight" to keep the internal sperm passages from becoming tangled! But today we know that while the scrotum does play two important roles, being a weight isn't one of them. First, this sac serves to hold and protect the delicate tissues of the testes. Second, it acts as a type of "thermostat" to make sure that the testes are always kept at about the same temperature. This temperature-control mechanism of the scrotum is worthy of a closer look.

A MAN'S REPRODUCTIVE PARTS AND THE ORGANS VERY NEAR THEM

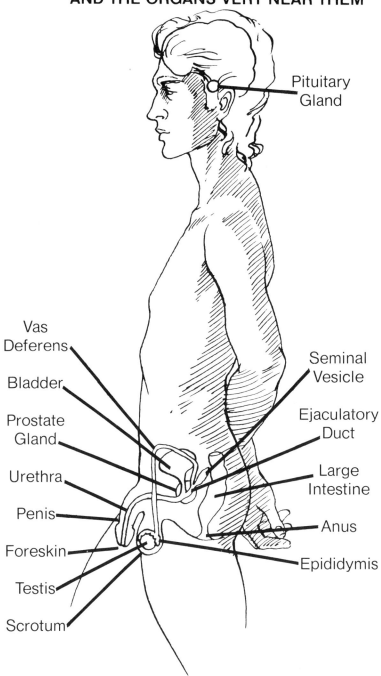

Pituitary Gland

Vas Deferens

Bladder

Prostate Gland

Urethra

Penis

Foreskin

Testis

Scrotum

Seminal Vesicle

Ejaculatory Duct

Large Intestine

Anus

Epididymis

In order for them to function properly, the testes must remain at a temperature some degrees *below* that of the rest of the body. The scrotum has a number of different sweat glands that constantly function to avoid any undesirable fluctuations. Additionally, the sac acts as a type of sling that can raise or lower the sex glands as necessary. If, for instance, you are outside in the bitter cold one winter day, the muscular portion of your scrotum will automatically raise your testes, bringing them closer to your body to maintain the ideal temperature. On the other hand, when you are in relatively warm surroundings, the muscles will become more relaxed, and the scrotum will lie as it usually does, loose and without any contact with your warm body. Sometimes men who wear jockey shorts or tight trousers interfere with the natural "thermostat" action of the scrotum—and find that the sperm-making process of the testes is interrupted. If these men are trying to become fathers, their doctors may recommend that they switch to looser clothing, to allow the sperm-making process to return to normal.

THE "SPERM PASSAGEWAYS"

As of this point, all we have talked about is the area of your body where sperm are made, that is, the testes that in turn are stored in the scrotum. But your reproductive apparatus is far more complicated than that. From the moment sperm are made, one could say they have one goal in mind: to get outside your body. In the process of making that great escape, they pass through an elaborate structure of "body highways," and while they are traveling, they pick up some very special liquid secretions. In the section below you will be reading about five portions of the sperm passageway, the (1) *epididymis,* (2) *vas deferens,* (3) *sperm "reservoir,"* (4) *ejaculatory duct,* and (5) *urethra* (you probably already know that the urethra runs through the penis). You will also be reading about two types of organs, the *prostate gland* and the *seminal vesicles,* which donate liquid additives to the sperm. As you can see from the opposite diagram, the sperm have to follow a rather complex route from the time they leave the testes until they are released through the tip of the penis.

EPIDIDYMIS: THE SPERM MATURING GROUNDS

The first part of the sperm-exiting process begins in the *epididymis*, which, as you can see in the diagram, is really an extension of the tubes of the testes. The mass of coils, which together look something like a comma, is twisted and irregular in shape, but if the coils were stretched out they would measure some sixteen to twenty feet.

The epididymis serves one very important purpose: It provides the ideal surroundings for new sperm to grow and mature before they continue on the journey that will eventually lead them to the outside of the body. When they first enter these coils, the sperm cells appear to be almost lifeless. In a matter of weeks, however, as a result of their exposure to the secretions of the walls of the epididymis, they come to life somewhat. We must say "somewhat," because compared to what they will be like later in their anatomical journey, the sperm when they leave the epididymis are still relatively sleepy cells.

THE PATH OF THE SPERM

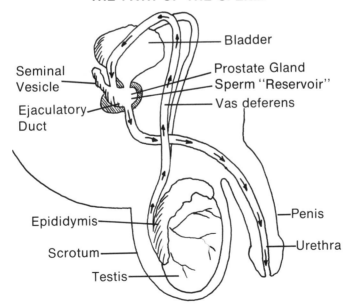

VAS DEFERENS: TUBES FOR TRAVELING

After approximately six weeks in the epididymis, the sperm enter the *vas deferens* (plural, *vasa deferentia*) or *ductus deferens*, a long, thick-walled tube that is specifically equipped to provide rapid transport for the sperm. As a result of the wavelike contractions of the muscular walls of the tubes and the gentle swaying of the *cilia* (the hairlike lining of the vas deferens), the sperm move gradually through the vas, all the way up to the abdominal area. Without this assistance from the cilia in the vas deferens, the young sperm cells would have a difficult time making this trip, since they just don't yet have enough of their own energy.

SPERM "RESERVOIR"

When the sperm complete the vas deferens run, they enter into a type of sperm "reservoir" or waiting room technically known as the *ampulla*. Here they wait until they get a release signal. Unlike their relatively long stay in the epididymis, sperm usually remain in the reservoir only for a short period of time.

THE "ESCAPE ROUTE": THE EJACULATORY DUCT AND URETHRA

When the right moment arrives, the sperm rush out of the reservoir into the *ejaculatory duct*, and eventually into the final part of the sperm passageway, the *urethra*.

You are probably already familiar with the word urethra, because it is not only part of your reproductive system, but it is an important structure in your urinary system as well. It is clear that nature was very economical in designing you. You must use your urethra for both conducting urine from your bladder and for conducting sperm from the internal sperm ducts to the outside world. Contrary to what you might think, the sperm do not get mixed up with the urine on the way out. Your body is equipped so that before sperm ever get into the urethra, special liquids cleanse the passageway and a valve near the bladder closes. In effect a roadblock is set up so that urine cannot pass through. Two pea-shaped glands known as *Cowper's glands* or *Bulbo-urethral glands*, which lie on either side of the urethra, play a particularly important role in preparing the urethra to receive sperm. They donate a sticky secretion that makes the tube an easier place for sperm to survive.

THOSE SECRETING STRUCTURES

You will recall that while the sperm were in the vas deferens, they were hardly the very peppy cells they are eventually supposed to be. They just responded to the contractions and pushes they received and slowly made their way along the passageways. But as the sperm are being released from the body, they receive contributions from some important structures, and they suddenly demonstrate a burst of energy.

Two *seminal vesicles*, both of which are pouchlike in shape and located near your bladder, release a special sugary type of liquid that mixes with the sperm. (The name "seminal vesicles" is hardly appropriate, given the role these organs play, but some scientists many years ago thought these pouches were little bladders to store sperm, and although we now know this is untrue, the name remains.) Once the seminal vesicles release their fluids, the sperm are awakened and they demonstrate an impressive ability to move by themselves.

The sperm also mix with a secretion from the *prostate gland*. This organ is a ring-shaped structure also located near your bladder. When you were born, it was as tiny as a grain of rice, but as you grew older, it enlarged and is now somewhere around the size of a chestnut. (This enlarging of the prostate continues throughout a man's life, and sometimes can be a problem. This is why doctors like to check the condition of the prostate gland to make sure that it doesn't become so big that it interferes with the passage of urine.)

The prostate gland has a contribution all its own: Its fluid not only helps sperm move, but also prepares them to survive if they ever get the opportunity to enter a woman's body.

THE PENIS

In this whole discussion, we have almost completely overlooked what seems to be the most obvious male reproductive structure, the *penis*, an organ that has two distinct functions: It allows the bladder to be emptied and it permits the introduction of sperm into a woman's body.

The penis, which usually lies in front of the scrotum (that is, when it is not stimulated), is covered with loose, highly elastic skin. Inside, it is filled with a mass of spongelike tissue that is capable of great expansion. The organ has two easily distinguishable parts: the body or *shaft*, which makes up most of the organ, and the head or *glans*, which contains a particularly rich supply of nerve endings and thus is highly susceptible to stimulation.

Many studies of the problems and concerns of young teenage boys (and even some who are *not* so young!) have shown that a substantial portion of them are worried that their penis is unusually small—or unusually large. This concern is not a new one. Medical history books are filled with examples of "recipes" that claimed to increase the size of a man's penis. In the 1600s, for instance, a newspaper carried an advertisement for a "magic treatment." A man responding to the notice wrote, "I have seen your advertisements in which you claim to increase the size of a small member. Perhaps you will kindly explain how this miracle is performed and whether you can guarantee one of giant proportions." The reply to this inquiry stated that the technique involved "washing, smoking and pulling." This report did not indicate whether the man actually went through with this "operation."

The average penis in an adult man when it is in a relaxed form is about three to four inches long. But "average" means that these measurements do not apply to every young man. Just as men vary in every other physical characteristic, they vary in the size of their sexual organs. And contrary to what you might hear from some of your friends, these differences in size are nothing to worry about. You can be sure, for instance, that penis size has absolutely nothing to do with sexual ability.

When a male baby is born, the glans, or end portion of his penis, is covered with a movable piece of skin in which there is an opening. This is the *foreskin*. For many hundreds of years, young boys in certain cultures (for instance the Jewish culture and a number of Near Eastern ones) have undergone a minor operation known as *circumcision*. The name for this surgical procedure comes from the Latin words for "cutting around," and that is exactly what circumcision is: cutting around and removing the foreskin.

In the United States—and in many other countries—circumcision has become an almost routine operation, which takes place in the hospital a few days after any boy is born. Most physicians now feel that circumcision is a good idea because the removal of this piece of skin allows a man to more easily wash away the normal type of secretions *(smegma)* that may collect at the tip of the penis. Furthermore, there is now evidence that men who are circumcised are much less likely to develop cancer of the penis (a very rare disease anyway), and women married to circumcised men are less likely to develop cancer of the cervix. (We'll discuss the cervix in Chapter 3.)

THE PITUITARY GLAND

Did you realize that not all of your important reproductive organs are located outside your body and in your pelvic region (the area just below your waist)? Did you know that one of your very important sex organs is located in the base of your *brain*? That's the *pituitary gland*, a bean-shaped organ, which in view of its many activities, is remarkably small.

The pituitary is involved in a wide variety of your body's functions. Indeed, because of its flexibility and tireless activity, it has been dubbed "the master gland." Actually the term "master gland" better describes the pituitary. As was the case with the seminal vesicles, some scientists many years ago misnamed this organ. Pituitary in Latin means "maker of mucus," and was applied to that little gland in the brain because it was believed that it was the source of nasal secretions!

During your childhood years, your master gland was very active in releasing chemical signals (hormones) into your bloodstream. These hormones played a part in the regulation of almost every one of your bodily functions—except those having to do with reproduction. Then, when you were about nine or ten, your master gland "woke up" with respect to its reproductive role and began to send out new hormonal signals. Of course you did not notice any signs of growing up right away—it took a few years for the pituitary hormones to get things started.

Why exactly your master gland suddenly becomes involved in reproductive activity at this age is not known. But from the moment it does, its secretions go right to work on your testes and other sexual equipment—and you are then on the path to manhood.

chapter 2

The Path to Manhood

FROM BOY TO MAN: THE GROWING-UP YEARS

So now you have some of the details about your complex reproductive anatomy. But you still need more facts about the types of physical changes that occur when a boy grows up, how the male sex cells are produced, and how all those millions of sperm are released from a man's body. Let's pick up from where we left off in the last chapter, with your master gland in your brain.

Hormonal Telegrams

It was your master gland that initiated your transition from boyhood to manhood. This organ sent out two different types of "hormonal telegrams," which had an immediate effect on many parts of your body. These two hormones are *ICSH* and *FSH*. You might think initially that we could refer to these as "male hormones," but we can't. These exact same secretions regulate the female reproductive system as well. Of course, what the master gland hormones *do* in the male body *is* distinctly masculine.

You can get an idea of what ICSH does just by looking at its full name: *interstitial-cell-stimulating hormone*. It stimulates cells—specifically, the interstitial cells in the tiny tubes of your testes. In order to get to these cells, ICSH must travel through the bloodstream, all the way from your brain to your pelvic region. And when it gets there, it causes those cells in your testes to produce a number of hormones, all of which together are known as *androgens*. The most important androgen is *testosterone*.

When your master gland sent out ICSH and your testes secreted increased amounts of testosterone, you began to notice some very important changes: Your sex organs, for instance, became larger and pubic hair started to grow in the lower part of your pelvic area. And this very male hormone did not limit itself to just one part of your body: It caused your bones to become heavier and longer, your muscles to expand significantly, and your skin to become thicker and tougher. With testosterone in your system, hair began to grow under your arms and on your face, legs, and chest. And your voice box became significantly larger (it is this change in your voice box and vocal cords that is responsible for that occasional embarrassing shift from a bellowing baritone to a squeaky soprano).

THE PITUITARY GLAND SENDS ICSH AND FSH THROUGH THE BLOODSTREAM TO THE TESTES

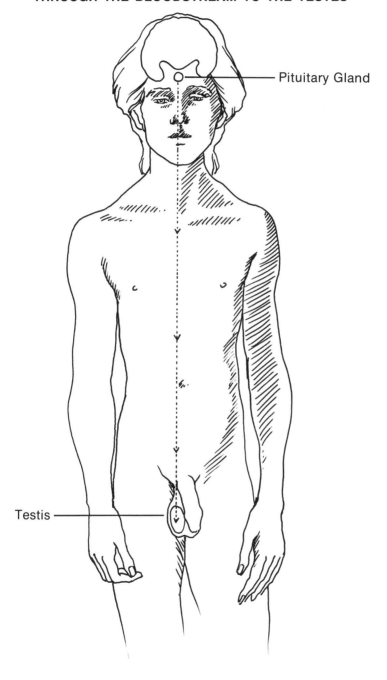

Pituitary Gland

Testis

FSH, the second master-gland hormone, is the abbreviation for *follicle-stimulating hormone.* In discussing ICSH we could get a clue as to its function by looking at its full name. But this is not the case with FSH. In the male body, FSH does *not* stimulate follicles. (The only reason it has this name is that the hormone was first identified in the female body, where it *does* stimulate follicles, and when it was learned that men have the identical hormone, scientists decided to keep the same name.)

In the male body, FSH travels from the brain to the testes to initiate the process of *spermatogenesis.* And this is a subject that merits a closer look.

Spermatogenesis

Spermatogenesis is the process during which sperm, or more technically, *spermatozoa,* are developed.

When FSH reaches the testes, it concentrates its efforts on the cells in the lining of those yards and yards of tubules you see in the opposite diagram. You have always had some "potential sperm cells" in the lining of these tubes, but throughout your childhood they were relatively inactive. FSH changes all of that. Somewhere between the ages of twelve and fifteen, your testes receive such a significant amount of stimulation from FSH that those dormant cells are awakened and the sperm-making process begins.

Spermatozoa do not just suddenly come into existence. They develop very gradually, following a regular pattern. What is particularly interesting about this pattern is that sperm cells develop in a manner *different from that of any other cell in the body.* You should know about three distinct phases in the sperm development process.

Step 1 of the sperm-making process starts just after some of the primitive cells (called spermatogonium) you had been carrying around in your testes divide and form other cells that look just like them. There is nothing unusual about this, because other cells in the body are constantly reproducing themselves—and the new cells that emerge look just like the old ones from which they came. In this case the new but still immature sperm cells (known as primary spermatocytes, only one of which is shown in the diagram) all carry the same type of cellular material (or chromosomes) as did

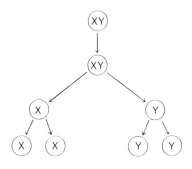

Spermatogonium

Step 1 (primary spermatocyte)

Step 2 (secondary spermatocytes)

Step 3 (spermatids)

the "parent cell." That means that this primitive sperm cell has *both* an X chromosome (which would make it a female-producing sperm) and a Y chromosome (which would make it a male-producing sperm).

It is during Step 2 that the really interesting things begin to happen. Here the primary spermatocyte, responding to the master-gland hormone FSH, does a very unusual thing: Instead of duplicating itself as all other cells do, it *splits into two different cells*, one of which carries a Y chromosome and one of which carries an X chromosome. At this point the growing sperm are called *secondary spermatocytes*, and they have only half the number of chromosomes that all other body cells have. These two "half cells" are identical except that one has a female-producing (X) sex chromosome and the other a male-producing (Y) sex chromosome.

In Step 3, each secondary spermatocyte splits into two identical *spermatids*, which don't reproduce but simply mature and become spermatozoa.

There are many more details that you could learn about the complex sperm-making process, but we will settle here for just four additional points.

First, spermatogenesis in each of its phases does not occur at the same time in all parts of your testes. Each of those yards of tubules have their own sperm-making schedule. In one tube phase 1 might be in process, in another phase 3 might be underway. But in all tubes, the growing sperm start out on the outside of the tubules and gradually are pushed closer and closer to the center of the tubes so that when the process is complete they will more easily be able to make their exit from the testes.

Second, spermatogenesis in a mature male does not just occur once in a while. Sperm-making is a *continuous* process, which begins at puberty and continues throughout a man's life (there is, however, some slowdown as a man gets older). This type of continuous production does not occur in all living creatures. Some male birds and other animals, for instance, produce sperm only during the autumn breeding season, thus ensuring that their young would only be born in the spring when the weather would be warm and pleasant and food would be plentiful. But mature human sperm—literally millions of them—are available all year round.

Third, the sperm-making process is very sensitive to certain conditions outside of a man's body. We've already talked about one of those conditions: excess heat. If the testes and scrotum are pushed up next to the warmth of a man's body, the ideal temperature for sperm-making would be altered, and the whole process could be affected. Similarly, scientists have shown that living at a high altitude and exposure to radiation or stress can interfere with normal spermatogenesis. During wars, for instance, pilot bombers who were sent on very dangerous and stressful missions often had trouble having offspring when they returned home. Usually, however, this slowdown in the sperm-making process is only a temporary one, and when the aggravating condition is eliminated, things return to normal.

Occasionally, however, sperm production is permanently affected. If, for instance, an adult male develops a severe case of mumps, his testes may be affected in a manner that interferes with sperm production. Because of this potential problem, many doctors urge parents to expose their sons to mumps so that can "get it over with" and not have to worry about possible problems later on.

Fourth, the process of spermatogenesis does not occur overnight. It takes a considerable amount of time for primitive sperm cells to become mature spermatozoa, about seventy-four days in adult men. Sperm production is a very complicated process and many different types of reproductive structures become involved. This point became particularly relevant when researchers started to look for ways of controlling sperm production in men. But you'll read about that in Chapter 6.

THE SPERM AND HOW THEY MAKE THEIR ESCAPE

The Male Sex Cell

If you had a very high-powered microscope and some slides and samples, you might be able to get a close-up look at some sperm cells. You would see right away that each of them looked like a tadpole, with a three-part structure. First there is an oval *head*, which contains the cell's nucleus and chromosomes, which will be a man's contribution to a new baby—if there is to be a baby. Then there is the *midsection*, which contains cytoplasm or the cell's storage and working area. Finally, there is the very distinctive long *tail*, which is capable of lashing movements and helps the sperm get where it wants to go.

The Travels of the Sperm

Let's quickly review the journey taken by the sperm from the time it is manufactured in the testes until it leaves the man's body.

You remember that as the sperm are produced in the tubules of the testes, they gradually move closer and closer to the middle of the tubes. Eventually, they are pushed into the epididymis, where they spend some time maturing. Then they enter the vas deferens and finally flow into the sperm reservoir, where they will wait patiently until they get the "release signal." But how are sperm released and when and where does it happen? Let's start with the "how."

Erection

Before any significant amount of sperm can be released from a man's body, a number of changes must take place within his reproductive system.

Either because of some outside type of stimulation, or maybe even for no external reason at all, his penis, which usually lies in a relaxed position, becomes filled with blood, that is, the man has an *erection*. You remember that the penis is made up of spongy material that allows it to change both in size and shape in a very short period of time. The events leading to these changes and the resulting erection are very complex and involve a whole cast of both nerves and muscles.

As we mentioned above, erections can occur for many different reasons—and in some very different circumstances. You might notice an erection after reading some sexy book or seeing a sexually provocative movie. On the other hand, you may have an erection when no sexual thoughts are involved—while swimming in cold water, when you are nervous, excited, or frightened about something, when you are wearing especially tight pants—or even when you are just waking up in the morning.

An erection may be brought about by psychological or physical factors. Similarly, a full bladder in the morning may create an internal situation that makes your penis erect.

Whatever the reason for the erection, it is certainly nothing to be concerned about. But some boys are. They are concerned that frequent and unexplained erections mean that they are "oversexed." And others are just worried that someone around them might notice. Of course it is ridiculous for them to be concerned about what is a very normal and natural process, a process that is very much part of being a man.

Ejaculation

After the penis has become erect, *ejaculation*, that is, the release of sperm from the male body, can occur. It *can* occur, but that does not mean it *has* to occur right then. A man may have an erection for a few minutes and then his penis may return to its normal, relaxed position.

If, however, there is further stimulation, and a complex set of messages is sent to the man's brain, the two-part process of ejaculation may occur. Once the process begins, both parts of it occur very quickly. In the *first* part of the ejaculation process, a large number of organs and muscles, including the prostate gland, seminal vesicles, and the sperm reservoir itself, begin to contract and literally push the waiting sperm toward the urethra. You remember, however, before they are ready to make their exit, the sperm need those extra chemical boosts. So, on their way out, they pick up the donations from the prostate gland and seminal vesicles and, by the time the sperm are pushed into the urethra, they are more than just "sperm." The cells plus the donations from the various male internal organs form a sticky, whitish fluid known as *semen*.

In the *second* part of the ejaculation, when the semen has entered the urethra, it is propelled by a series of contractions that involve practically all the muscles in the man's pelvic region. When the semen makes its exit, it does so in five to seven quick spurts over a five-to-ten second period, and the penis becomes relaxed again.

It has been estimated that during each ejaculation, between 66 and 867 million sperm are released. But even with these millions of cells, the semen would fill only barely one teaspoon. There are significantly more sperm cells in the first part of the ejaculated semen than in the part released later—or in the second ejaculation, if one occurs a short time later.

The moment of release is a very pleasurable one for the man and brings with it a wide variety of sensations that affect his entire body. The whole experience, including the release of the semen and the sensations, is referred to as *orgasm*. There appears to be a relationship between the amount of semen released and the satisfaction a man achieves from orgasm. He might find particularly that a second ejaculation, if it occurs very soon after the first one, may not be as satisfying as the first.

So far we have been discussing *how* erection and ejaculation occur. But when and where do these events take place?

Seminal Emissions

The testes produce so many sperm—literally millions each day—and the sperm reservoir just isn't large enough to accommodate an unlimited number of them. Eventually, they have to get out. Some small number of the "excess" sperm gradually pass out unnoticed with urine. But the great majority of them remain until the pressure becomes so great that they are released automatically.

The first automatic release a boy experiences usually occurs in his sleep and so it is called a *nocturnal emission* or *wet dream*. This type of expulsion of semen may follow a sexy dream—but then it may happen without this stimulation. In either event, nocturnal emissions are perfectly normal and represent the body's way of providing fresh sperm to the reservoir.

One young boy may have his first emission at age twelve or even sooner. Another may not experience a wet dream until age fifteen or later. The average age at first emission is about thirteen and a half, but there is a great deal of room for difference around that average. Once the first ejaculation occurs, a boy can expect that it will happen fairly regularly—maybe once a week or maybe once a month.

Although there is no argument today about the fact that seminal emissions in young men are perfectly normal events, many boys still believe the old stories to the effect that wet dreams mean that your manliness is "flowing out." Others feel guilty about the ejaculations and worry that their parents might see the stains on the bed sheets and "find out." Still others, who may not have been told what wet dreams are and why they occur, may be very frightened.

All their concerns, of course, are without cause, since these spontaneous ejaculations, far from being a threat to their "manliness," are actually a sure sign that their male reproductive system is becoming fully developed and mature. And since parents *know* that their sons are approaching young adulthood, they expect that these ejaculations will occur.

Masturbation

Almost all—if not all—young men masturbate, that is, they manipulate their own sex organs, often to the point of bringing about an ejaculation.

Throughout history there have been all types of strange and untrue stories about masturbation and the alleged problems it can cause for young men practicing it. Just fifty years ago, some misled parents would grimly warn their sons to "not play with your tassel, or it will fall off!" Or they would claim that this form of "self-abuse" and "self-pollution" would cause acne, heart disease, and worst of all, mental illness. The concern about masturbation as a cause of mental illness stemmed from the report of some medical people who observed that patients in mental hospitals were masturbating. They concluded that these two factors must be linked.

But today masturbation is recognized as a normal form of sexual behavior among teenage boys—and even among grown men. Psychiatrists and psychologists feel that masturbation becomes excessive only when it becomes a preoccupation—that is, when it begins to interfere with other aspects of a young man's life. (These professionals point out that when carried to an extreme, masturbation is probably a symptom of some deeper emotional disturbance.) But this happens *very* rarely. For the great majority of boys, masturbation should be accepted as natural and normal, and doctors emphasize that boys should *not* feel guilty about it.

Sexual Intercourse

When a man's penis becomes firm and erect, it can be inserted into a woman's sex organ, that is, her vagina. If there is sufficient stimulation (from the continued contact of the penis and the walls of her vagina), ejaculation can occur and millions of sperm are released into her body.

Among married men, sexual intercourse (this process is also known as coitus or copulation) is the primary way sperm are released from their bodies (although even when they are married, most men continue to have seminal emissions, and some of them may masturbate occasionally). But sexual intercourse for a young, unmarried man carries with it some unique and far-reaching consequences—the types of consequences that do not accompany either seminal emissions or masturbation. The most obvious consequence of sexual intercourse is the possibility of a new life being created. This is one reason why most young men—even though they are physically mature and fully capable of participating in both sexual intercourse and the reproductive process—want to postpone this experience until a time when they can fully enjoy it and accept the responsibilities that go with it. (You'll read more about this subject in Chapters 7 and 8.)

chapter 3

When a Girl Grows Up

FROM GIRL TO WOMAN

You first began to notice the signs of your transition to manhood when you were around twelve, thirteen, or fourteen years old. But you probably were aware that the girls in your class at school began to develop about a year—or maybe even more—before you and your friends did. It is a medical fact that females begin their physical transition to adulthood earlier than males. Of course, when males *do* start the growth process, they develop at a truly fantastic pace and quickly surpass their female counterparts in terms of height and weight.

You should be aware of the names and locations of some of the important female reproductive organs and about the details of the uniquely female process of *menstruation*.

You know that a significant number of your sexual organs—your testes, scrotum, and penis, for instance—are located outside of your body. In women, however, the great majority of sexual organs are found inside their bodies in a cagelike structure formed by their two hipbones. You've probably noticed that the hipbones of mature women are relatively wider than a man's. This enables them to accommodate all those delicate internal organs—and, of course, it allows for the possibility that some day they may be carrying a growing baby inside of them.

Ovaries—The Egg Producers

You can think of the internal female reproductive organs as being distributed within the pelvic area in the shape of a large Y with curved arms. At the tip of these arms are two almond-shaped glandular organs known as *ovaries*. The ovaries are often referred to as the "primary female sex glands" and they represent the woman's equivalent to your testes. A female's ovaries develop during her prenatal life from the same type of cellular tissue that formed your testes. For her, it was the existence of an X or female-producing chromosome from her father's sperm cell that determined that the mass of cells would develop in a way which would make her female.

The name "ovaries" (from the Latin word *ova*, meaning eggs)

A WOMAN'S REPRODUCTIVE PARTS AND THE ORGANS VERY NEAR THEM

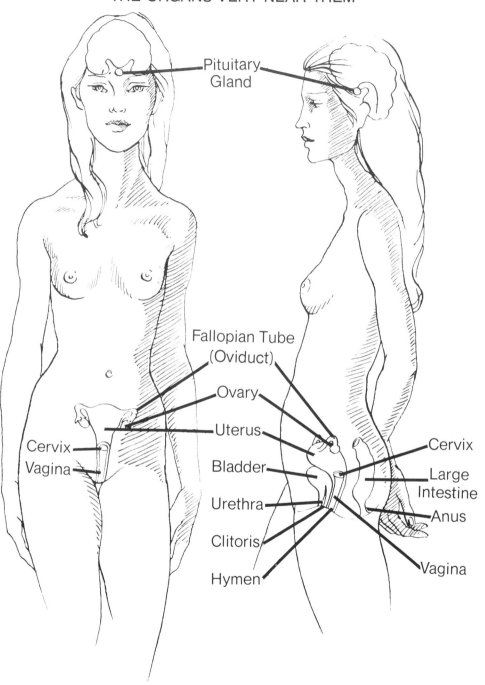

gives you a pretty good clue as to the type of activity in which the female sex glands participate: The two ovaries produce the egg cells, or ova (singular, ovum), which when united with male sperm have the capability of developing into a new human being.

There are many differences between the egg-producing and sperm-producing processes, and we will get to some of the details of those differences in a later section. But here it is important to point out that while you, as a new young man, will be constantly manufacturing sperm throughout your whole life, a female is born with her lifetime supply of eggs. She never manufactures any more.

It has been estimated that a girl baby at birth may have up to a half a million eggs in her ovaries. In the course of her first ten or so years, this number is considerably diminished, but she still has an incredible number of egg cells left by the time she reaches maturity—maybe some 200,000–400,000 of them, all so small you would need a microscope to see them. Theoretically, each cell is capable of joining with a sperm cell to form a baby, but in reality, only about three or four hundred eggs are ever released from her ovaries in the course of her lifetime, and there are definite biological limits on how many children a woman can have. (Most women have no intention of trying to find out what that limit is!)

Tubes for Transport

Just as male sperm have an "anatomical highway" to travel on after they are released from the testes, so does the female egg have such a structure that receives it after the release from the ovary: These structures, which correspond to the two curved arms in the Y structure, are called the *fallopian tubes*, or *oviducts*. Each of these tubes is about four inches long and about as wide as a telephone cord. And as the vas deferens and its internal hairlike cilia provide a form of "rapid transport" for the sperm, the fallopian tubes (both of which are located adjacent to the ovaries, but not connected to them) draw the egg in and gently propel it along. The egg cannot move by itself. It just drifts along following whatever currents the cilia provide. And all those currents push the little egg toward a structure known as the *uterus*.

The Pear-Shaped Organ

Looking again at that large Y, you can think of the uterus (also known as the womb) as being located in the area above where the two arms meet. Where before we could point to some general types of similarities between the testes and ovaries and the vas deferens and fallopian tube, we cannot here. The uterus is a uniquely feminine structure.

There are many facts about the uterus that you should be familiar with, but at this point, let's concentrate on just four of them.

First, the size of the uterus varies. In women who have not had children it is about the size of your clenched fist. In women who have had one or more children, it is somewhat larger. Second, the uterus has a special type of lining called the *endometrium*. At one point a woman's endometrium is richly lined with blood and other tissue cells and would make an ideal place for an egg that has joined with a sperm to settle and begin to grow. At other times, the uterine lining is bare, having lost its accumulation of blood and other tissue.

Third, and very important, the uterus, which you know is the organ in which a growing baby develops, has an incredible capacity for expansion. During pregnancy this organ can increase up to five-hundred times its original size. You can get an idea of the magnitude of the growth in this organ by looking again at your clenched fist and imagining how much larger that organ would have to become in order to hold an eight- or nine-pound baby.

Fourth, the uterus, which is shaped something like an upside-down pear, has a tiny opening in its lower part. This opening, or *cervix*, is very firm and made up of highly muscular material and is so small that ordinarily something as small as a pencil could hardly go through it. But under great pressure, that is, when a baby is about to be born, the cervix has the remarkable capacity to stretch so much that the infant can pass through during the birth process.

The Vagina—A Connection with the Outside World

The cervix connects the uterus with the vagina, a tubular structure that is about four inches long. The vagina is both a woman's sexual organ and is the birth canal through which a new baby can pass from the uterus to the outside world.

The inner wall of the vagina is composed of highly elastic small folds or ridges that allow this female organ to stretch during both sexual intercourse and childbirth. The vagina is kept clean and moist by tiny glands in its inner walls, which continuously produce a cleansing and lubricating film. *Bartholin's glands* on both sides of the vaginal opening contribute additional lubrication when a woman becomes sexually stimulated.

In identifying exactly where in a woman's body the vagina is located, it is useful to consider the two other openings she has in her genital area: the urethra and anus. The vagina is located between those two structures. You recall that men use their urethra for two purposes—to conduct both urine and sperm. But the woman is different here in that her sexual and urinary organs are completely separate. The only thing they have in common is their nearby position in her anatomy.

Some women have a membranelike structure, the *hymen*, that may cover or partially cover the opening to the vagina. For ages people believed that the presence of this hymen was a sure sign that a female was a virgin, that is, that she had not yet had sexual intercourse. But it is now known that the hymen—or the lack of a hymen—is not a reliable sign of sexual experience. Some girls break their hymens during physical activity—some girls never had one. It seems that the hymen throughout history has been given much more attention than it merits.

A Female's Outside Parts

Not all of a woman's reproductive and sexual organs are in the internal Y structure. Her vagina and urethra both open out into an area called the *external genitalia*, the catchall name for a number of different structures.

The *mons pubis* is a cushionlike mound of fat, covered with pubic hair and located in her pelvic region. Right below the mons pubis is a small pea-shaped structure called the *clitoris*. This tiny organ is made up of many nerve receptors and other sensitive tissues. When a woman becomes sexually excited, her clitoris becomes filled with blood (similar to what happens to your penis when it is stimulated), is very much increased in size, and plays a major role in female orgasm. For these reasons, the clitoris is considered to be the female counterpart to the male penis. But the comparison cannot be drawn too far, because the clitoris does not release any type of secretion, as the penis does during ejaculation. Nor, as we will discuss later, is female orgasm necessary for a pregnancy to occur.

The external genitalia also includes the *labia majora* (or "large lips"), two rounded folds of skin that extend from the mons pubis. Inside these "large lips" are the *labia minora*, or small lips. When a woman is sexually aroused, these small lips, as well as her clitoris, respond and significantly increase in size.

The Female Breasts

One of the early signs of a girl's growing up is the development of her breasts. Breasts appear in both males and females, but only in women do they begin to grow as adulthood approaches. But how do the breasts function?

The most obvious portions of the female breast are the *nipple* and the pigmented area around the nipple known as the *areola*. The mass of these organs consists of cushions of fat, which cover the important glands known as the *mammary glands*. When they are stimulated by an infant's sucking on the nipple of the breast, milk is secreted in sufficient supply to give the baby a completely nourishing diet—and a form of protection against certain diseases. Under some conditions, the female breasts can secrete up to a quart of milk, or more, every day to feed a hungry infant— that is, if the mother *chooses* to take advantage of this natural food supply. Some mothers do; some mothers don't. It's a matter of choice.

While milk secretion is the true function of the female breasts, these organs are important in other ways. First, breasts are very responsive to sexual stimulation. At this time the nipples become more erect and the size of the breasts increase somewhat. Second, for some people—both men and women—the size and shape of the female breast is a particular topic of interest and an important part of female sexuality. Some women feel so insecure about the size of their breasts that they undergo surgical procedures—to either increase or decrease their size or in some other way alter the appearance of these structures.

Actually, however, for a young woman to worry about the size of her breasts is about as unnecessary as it is for a boy to worry over the size of his penis. As with most characteristics of humans, there is a natural range of difference. Breast size is generally determined by hereditary and/or nutritional factors that determine how much fat tissue is present. Additionally, breast size will vary over the course of a woman's life—and the size has nothing directly to do with her sexuality.

The Master Gland

You recall that all your outward signs of maturity—your increase in height and weight, the growth of your sex organs, your voice change—just to name a few—came about after your pituitary gland sent the hormonal telegrams FSH and ICSH to your testes. A girl's transition to womanhood is triggered by the exact same hormones. But in her body, the timetable for their release is different. In your case, FSH and ICSH are released at about the same time and your master gland keeps producing them regularly throughout your adult life. In the female, however, these hormones are released sequentially that is one after the other and they are secreted in significant quantities only for some thirty or thirty-five years of her life. In her case, FSH is the first master-gland signal sent out.

FSH—The Female "Grow Up" Signal

The girl-to-woman transition schedule is something like this: FSH is released when the girl is about eight or nine. She doesn't notice effects right away, but actually, this master-gland signal causes her ovaries to begin producing increasing amounts of the hormone *estrogen*. And it is estrogen that does for her what testosterone did for you, that is, it initiates the transition to adulthood.

Around age ten or eleven, she notices that her breasts are becoming fuller and her hips are widening. She has a rapid spurt in height and an increase in weight. Pubic hair begins to grow in the shape of an upside-down triangle in her lower pelvic region. And then, at approximately age twelve and a half, this new young woman experiences the most significant of all her physical changes: She has her first menstrual period.

THE MENSTRUAL CYCLE

Menstruation is the process whereby a small amount of blood (usually about two or three ounces) is released from a woman's uterus, through her vagina to the outside of her body. It's a complex process, one that involves many different organs and hormones. But it is important that you read about these complexities in order that you can better understand the details of human reproduction and its control.

You remember that earlier in this chapter we pointed out that the uterus has a very special type of lining known as the endometrium. At one point this endometrium is filled with blood and tissue cells and would make an ideal place for a baby to grow. When no baby presents himself or herself, this lining is not needed, and is gradually released from the woman's body. And this is the menstrual flow.

But how is this rich uterine lining ever built up in the first place? And how does the woman's body know when it is time to release it? The key to the answers to these questions lies in the events of the *menstrual cycle.*

First of all, do you know what a cycle is? It is a series of changes that occur in a fairly regular manner, time and time again, each time returning to the same starting point. Take the seasons of the year, for instance. Spring is followed by summer, summer by fall, fall by winter, and then you are back to spring again. This is a cycle. The tide of the sea ebbs and flows in a constant, natural rhythm. And this is a cycle too. The events that occur within a mature woman's body about every twenty-eight days make up another cycle, the menstrual cycle.

But the menstrual cycle is different from that of the seasons and the tides. First, the menstrual cycle has a limited period of time during which it occurs, usually from about age twelve or thirteen (or whenever a woman has her first menstrual flow) until about age forty-five or fifty. Second, there are many aspects of this cycle that are not always the same from woman to woman. Even within the same woman, the timing of cycle events can be different from month to month.

As we already pointed out, the usual age at which the first menstrual period occurs is about twelve and a half. But, just as there is variation in the age at which a young man has his first seminal emission, there is also a variation in the timing of the onset of menstruation in women. Some young women have their first periods at age nine or even earlier. Others do not experience menstruation until age sixteen. It is all a matter of a woman's individual "body timetable."

Similarly, most women have a menstrual period about once every twenty-eight days. But again there can be variation in the number of days between periods. A girl can be perfectly normal with a twenty-four-day cycle, or a thirty-five-day cycle, or if she does not always have the same cycle length. Usually women develop a timing pattern after they have had their periods for a few years. But many external events—a trip across country, concern about an exam, excitement over a party, for instance—can throw off a previously regular schedule.

THE TWO MOST IMPORTANT CYCLE EVENTS

Whatever the length of her menstrual cycle, a woman experiences two distinct and very important biological events. The first one, which we have already briefly discussed, is menstruation, the release of the lining of the uterus. The second one is *ovulation*, the release of a mature egg from the woman's ovary.

Ovulation is something that scientists have been able to understand—if only vaguely—for many years. Just as they understood that the male body produced sperm cells and released them from time to time, it seemed logical that the female body also occasionally would release a type of "reproductive cell." But what they couldn't understand was menstruation. "Why," they asked, "does a woman bleed about once a month?"

Some early doctors "explained" that women bleed regularly because they were bitten by serpents or some supernatural animals. Others thought that because the cycle occurred about once every twenty-eight days, women were in some way "under the influence of the moon," since the moon also went through phases in about the same length of time.

When no one could come up with an acceptable explanation, people concluded that the process of menstruation was not only mysterious, but also magical. Women were bleeding—but they were completely healthy! This appeared to be contradictory, so it was widely assumed that women during these days had other types of strange powers. Some observers claimed that menstruating women could turn beverages sour, cause jam to spoil, and plants to die. In some cultures, menstruating women were not allowed to come near men, lest they cast some type of "evil female spell."

The most popular nineteenth- and early twentieth-century explanation of why menstruation occurred was that, just as a man has seminal emissions to release his sperm, a woman has a menstrual flow to release her egg. As late as 1920 this belief prevailed. But it was wrong! An almost complete understanding of the menstrual cycle has now demonstrated that menstruation and ovulation occur in *two different* parts of the cycle.

In considering these two separate events—and those associated with them—it is useful for us to think of the menstrual cycle as being a wheel that is divided into three unequal parts. The first part is the menstrual flow itself. The second part includes all those events that occur before ovulation. The third part includes all those events that occur after ovulation and before the next menstrual flow.

THE PARTS OF A 28-DAY MENSTRUAL CYCLE

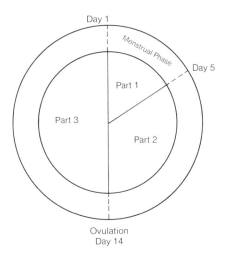

PART 1 OF THE MENSTRUAL CYCLE:
THE MENSTRUAL PHASE

Two important events occur during the first part of the menstrual cycle. First, the blood and tissue lining of the endometrium is released from the woman's body. Second, that master-gland hormone FSH is released in increasing quantities, and has the effect of starting the cycle all over again. Let's pause for a moment to consider the menstrual flow and how a young woman reacts to it.

The onset of her first menstrual flow is an important event in the life of a girl—in a sense, like the first seminal emission for a young man. Both events dramatically illustrate that the transition to adulthood is well under way. If a girl is not prepared for the onset of her first period, she may be very concerned. Since bleeding is usually associated with sickness, unless she has advance information she may begin to worry. When she has the facts, however, a woman becomes fully aware that her menstrual flow is indeed a sign of health, and an indication that her reproductive system is developing normally.

When the bleeding begins, a girl has a choice of a number of products that will serve to catch and absorb the menstrual flow as it is released. One type of protection is a *sanitary pad*, which can be held in place by pins, belts, or a variety of other means. Another type is a *tampon*, a form of "internal protection." The tampons are designed so that, once they are in place, she is not aware of their presence. There used to be some hesitation about young girls using tampons, but now it is widely agreed that women of all shapes, sizes, and ages can use them very successfully.

You may hear menstruation being referred to as "the curse." This is because some women do have minor problems during their periods. A girl, for instance, may have menstrual cramps in the lower part of her abdomen (technically known as *dysmenorrhea*). Although most women experience some discomfort at one time or another during their menstrual period, only in severe cases will a doctor's help be necessary. In addition to cramps, some women complain of feeling irritable, "snappy," or maybe just a little bit sad right before or during their periods. Physicians refer to this syndrome as *premenstrual tension*, a condition that may be related to the change in the level of female hormones and increased water retention about this time.

As you will read in the next part of this chapter, unlike men, women have fluctuations in the level of their various hormones. There is medical evidence that the shifts in their hormones during the menstrual cycle can have an effect on their attitudes and behaviors. These are not *major* changes, but a woman may very well be more sensitive during one portion of her cycle—particularly during those days just before the menstrual flow starts.

FSH Starts Things All Over Again

A couple of days after the menstrual flow begins, while a woman is still in Part 1 of her menstrual cycle, her master gland gets the whole cycle going again by releasing FSH into her bloodstream. As soon as her ovaries receive this hormonal message, a number of eggs begin to grow. Usually only one egg plays the leading role in each cycle, but for some reason a few eggs in each ovary begin to grow after they are stimulated by FSH.

Not only do these few chosen eggs begin to grow within a protective structure known as the follicle, but these follicles start to produce estrogen, the hormone that played such an important role in changing a girl into a woman. This important hormone also plays a critical role in the continuation of menstrual cycle events and one of the first items on estrogen's list of "things to do" is to get to work rebuilding the lining of the uterus, which was just released during the menstrual flow.

PART 2 OF THE MENSTRUAL CYCLE: THE EVENTS THAT OCCUR BEFORE OVULATION

During this phase of the cycle, the estrogen acts on the uterus to ensure that it continues its growth of blood and tissue layers. At the same time, the eggs in the ovary continue to grow. At first, each of the selected eggs is made up of one layer of cells. As this second menstrual-cycle phase continues, however, each of these tiny eggs begins to grow and becomes surrounded by a thick, protective membrane.

Enter, Hormone LH!

Near the end of this second-cycle phase, about the thirteenth or fourteenth day of a twenty-eight-day menstrual cycle, the master gland sends out another hormonal message to the ovary. This hormone is the *luteinizing hormone,* abbreviated, LH. The reason the master gland sends out LH at this exact moment appears to be related to the amount of estrogen that has accumulated in the body. A woman's system has a type of built-in thermostat that controls the release of hormones. Just as a thermostat heater turns itself on and off as the temperature in the room fluctuates, the female body's thermostat, in this case, releases LH when a certain level of estrogen is attained.

The name of the hormone LH may be unfamiliar to you, but actually you have read about it before. LH is *exactly the same* as your hormone ICSH, that secretion which in your body is so important in stimulating your testes to produce testosterone. But in the female, this hormone was given another name.

"Luteinizing" is a word derived from the Latin word for "yellow." And, as is so often the case with medical terminology, the

THE LEVELS OF ESTROGEN AND PROGESTERONE DURING A MENSTRUAL CYCLE

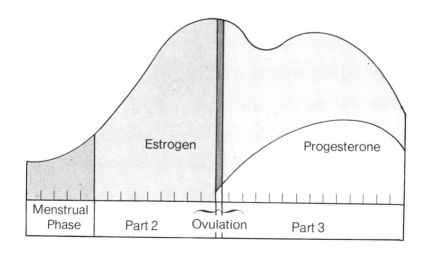

term *luteinizing hormone* describes what this secretion does—
that is, it describes *one* of the things LH does.

LH has a number of important functions. First, it appears to be
responsible for choosing the one of these twenty or so growing
eggs that will be released into the woman's fallopian tube during
this cycle. Usually just one egg is chosen. Occasionally more than
one is released and then all kinds of interesting things (described in
Chapter 4) can happen. Once the selection is made, the rest of
these eggs disintegrate.

Second, LH triggers the release of the chosen mature egg from
its follicle and changes the follicle into a bright yellow-orange
structure (this is how LH got its name). This new structure,
known as the *corpus luteum*, or *yellow body*, will produce a new
type of female hormone. All of these events occur during and just
after ovulation (a process that we will examine more closely in the
next chapter).

PART 3 OF THE MENSTRUAL CYCLE:
THE EVENTS TAKING PLACE AFTER OVULATION

Once the egg has escaped from the ovary and the follicle in which it
grew, it is really on its own. The egg is very different from the
sperm in that it cannot move by itself. Right after ovulation the
fringes of the fallopian tubes (which, you remember, are located
very near the ovaries) begin to wave around and actually draw the
egg into their funnel-like opening. Once in the tube, the egg is
gently bounced up and down and moved along by the hairlike cilia.
These cilia are very much like the cilia in your vas deferens that
generally propel sperm on their way.

Progesterone—The Second Important Female Hormone

When the hormone LH changes the former follicle into a yellow
body, this structure begins to secrete the second important female
hormone, *progesterone*. Progesterone teams up with estrogen to
complete the building up of the lining of the uterus. Remember
that just as progesterone is being secreted, the egg is already
making its way down the fallopian tube. It takes only about four or
six days to make that journey, so time is running short. Proges-

terone has to work very efficiently with estrogen to make sure the accommodations in the uterus are ideal—in case the egg meets a sperm in its journey.

Progesterone does a couple of different things for the uterus that estrogen alone could not do. For instance, normally the uterus is likely to contract once in a while. If a new baby is going to settle and grow there, it could hardly rest comfortably if these contractions were to continue, so progesterone goes to work to relax the uterus for approximately the next two weeks so that it will truly be an ideal place for the baby to grow—if there is to be a baby. Additionally, while estrogen focused its efforts on the tissues of the womb, progesterone specializes in developing the glands of the uterus. These glands will be able to secrete materials that will provide nourishment for a baby.

Within about a week or so after ovulation, the lining of the uterus is all set to perform its important and specialized function, that is, it is ready to receive a fertilized egg. But for the majority of cycles in a woman's life, no fertilized egg arrives and the uterus receives no chemical pregnancy signal.

AND ANOTHER CYCLE COMES TO AN END

In the absence of this signal, the high levels of estrogen and progesterone in the bloodstream signal the pituitary gland to stop producing the hormone LH. Without LH, the yellow body, that transformed follicle, can no longer produce its two important hormones. Without high levels of estrogen and progesterone, which were so important in building up the lining of the uterus, the accumulated blood and tissues begin to deteriorate. The tissue layers and menstrual blood begin to gently flow out of the uterus, through the vagina. And the menstrual period begins.

As we already said, during most menstrual cycles of a woman's life, no fertilized egg arrives in the uterus. But occasionally one does—and that means a pregnancy is in process. Chapter 4 will tell you about that subject.

chapter 4

When the Sperm and the Egg Become One

BEYOND THE STORK THEORY

As you can tell from reading the first three chapters on the structure and function of the male and female reproductive systems, we now have a detailed understanding of how our sex organs work, and how nature has designed our bodies so that they can make their own unique contribution to the process of reproduction. Of course, we still don't have the answers to *all* the questions, but we do for many of them. But this advanced state of knowledge should not be taken for granted. Serious research into human reproductive physiology is something very new, and only relatively recently in human history did the facts begin to accumulate.

Until well into this century, just about all the topics related to sex and reproduction were clouded by mystery and suspicion. There was a vague yet persistent feeling that this category of subject matter was not worthy of study and investigation. So medical scientists focused on every system of the body *except* the reproductive system. High school students would be given biology books that only vaguely referred to the manner in which new life was brought into the world.

Those who did venture into this "forbidden research area" were severely criticized. In 1676, when Leeuwenhoek, with his newly discovered microscope, identified sperm in male semen, many of his fellow scientists were horrified, pointing out that he was "breaching morality." In 1787, the headmaster of a German school published an essay entitled "The Newly Revealed Mystery of Nature in the Structure and Fertilization of Flowers," in which he described the reproductive process in higher plants. His associates were shocked over his "indiscretion." Very quickly he lost his teaching post and his "nasty" book was withdrawn from circulation.

And this general attitude prevailed into this century. In the early 1900s a Chicago physician delivered a paper on "sexual problems in marriage" at a medical convention. His fellow doctors thought the paper was "disgraceful" and refused to allow him to publish it in their association's medical journal.

With this feeling that sex and reproductive research was wrong, and indeed shocking, it is hardly surprising that we had to cope for many hundreds of years with a wide variety of sexual myths. Children grew up being told that the stork brought them, or that they came about when their mother swallowed a seed, or when they were purchased in a hospital's baby shop. The whole subject was very mysterious—not only to the young adults who were asking the questions, but also in many cases to the parents who were supposed to be providing the answers.

But today things are different. We have more facts than ever before, and we are less hesitant to talk about these facts. The story of the creation of a new human life is one of the most complex and fascinating ones you could ever read about. And this whole reproductive drama focuses on the male sperm and the female egg, the two little cells that eventually get together to form one. Let's take a closer look at both of them.

THOSE TWO REPRODUCTIVE CELLS

You already know a great deal about the spermatozoa, how they are produced, what they look like, and the road they follow in making the great escape from your body. Similarly, you have some general background about the female egg and how it is released from the ovary into the fallopian tube. But what is of particular interest here are some of the more detailed aspects of these two types of cells, the major differences between them, and the effect

THE TWO REPRODUCTIVE CELLS

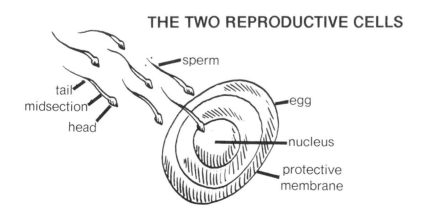

these differences have in determining the time and place of their potential rendezvous.

Size and Shape

Spermatozoa are the smallest cells in the human body. It has been estimated that it would take over six hundred of them placed head to tail to equal just one inch. But what they lack in size, they make up in number. There are so many sperm released in just one ejaculation (somewhere between 66 and 867 *million* of them) that if they were placed head to tail they would stretch for miles.

In size, the female egg is as different as it could be from the male sperm. The egg is the *largest* cell in the human body, about as large as the period at the end of this sentence. And instead of there being millions of them present, there is usually just one mature egg available during each menstrual cycle.

The sperm's head, which makes up about one-tenth of the length of the cell, contains the nucleus and the twenty-three chromosomes, that is, the hereditary materials that make up the father's contribution to the child. Behind the head is the midsection, which contains the storage and working materials for the cell to use in the course of its journey through the sperm's passageways into the woman's body. Finally, there is the tail, which is able to propel the entire cell with whipping motions. Scientists have documented that in favorable conditions a sperm can move at the rate of about seven inches an hour.

Now compare the structure of the sperm to that of the egg. The female cell not only looks like a monster next to the sperm (it is estimated that by volume the egg is 85,000 times as large as the sperm), but also has a completely different shape. Like the sperm, the egg has a nucleus with twenty-three chromosomes, which reflect the inheritable characteristics of the woman. The nucleus is surrounded by *cytoplasm*, or the egg's "yolk," which contains, among other things, some nutritive material that will be useful to the egg during its journey down the fallopian tube. Surrounding the egg's yolk is a transparent protective membrane known as the *zona pellucida*. Before the egg and sperm can get together, this protective membrane must be penetrated so that the nucleus of the sperm and the nucleus of the egg can merge to form one.

The Life Span of the Egg and Sperm

The female egg cell has a relatively short lifetime. If it does not meet a sperm sometime during the first twenty-four hours or so after it leaves the ovary, it will simply disintegrate. Some medical researchers feel that the egg will disintegrate even *earlier* than this, possibly even within twelve hours after it leaves the ovary. During these twelve to twenty-four hours of free floating, the egg does not get much beyond the outer third of the fallopian tube. And that is where the meeting of the egg and sperm usually takes place, that is, if it happens at all.

But again, the sperm cells are very different from the egg. They can survive longer once they are released from a man's body. Sperm probably maintain their ability to fertilize an egg for about forty-eight hours. We say "probably" because this is a very difficult subject to study in human beings, since it requires finding and examining sperm that already have completed the trip to the woman's fallopian tubes. Doctors who have examined women have found sperm alive and moving in their tubes after ninety-six hours or longer, but they suspect that these sperm had, by that time, lost so much of their energy that they could not join successfully with an egg.

When Can Pregnancy Occur?

Knowing that the sperm can function for about forty-eight hours inside a woman's body, and the egg for about twenty-four hours, we can calculate the approximate number of hours during one menstrual cycle when sexual intercourse could lead to pregnancy: About seventy-two hours, that is, three consecutive twenty-four-hour periods that may cover parts of four days. We add these two time periods because sperm have the capacity to survive some forty-eight hours to await the arrival of the egg. If, for instance, a woman has intercourse on Monday night and releases her egg on Wednesday night, some sperm may still be available to fertilize it.

48 hours	24 hours	72 hours
approximate fertilization capacity of the sperm	+ approximate survival interval of the egg	= approximate time during each menstrual cycle when intercourse could lead to pregnancy

But which four days? How would a husband and wife go about identifying the time of the wife's cycle when pregnancy might occur?

It is easy to give a superficial answer to that question: Pregnancy has the greatest chance of occurring on those days when both an egg and a sufficient number of sperm are present at the same time in the woman's body. But the detailed answer that you need is more complex. We *know* when sperm are present. They enter the woman's body after sexual intercourse. But we don't always know exactly when the egg is going to be present.

The Timing of Ovulation

The female egg is released from the ovary on about the fourteenth or fifteenth day of a twenty-eight-day menstrual cycle. It is necessary to say "about" because even today, with our sophisticated instruments and knowledge, scientists do not know exactly when ovulation occurs. Some women do have physical signs of ovulation: They may experience a sharp pain in their abdomen (called *mittelschmerz*), which may correspond to the release of the egg; or a woman may notice a whitish secretion being released from her vagina on the day just preceding ovulation. But generally, it is much easier for doctors and women themselves to know that ovulation *has* occurred, and more difficult to say when it *will* occur or when it *is* occurring.

It is generally believed that a woman releases an egg about *fourteen days before the last day of her menstrual cycle.* Technically, scientists feel that ovulation occurs somewhere in the interval twelve to sixteen days before the beginning of the next menstrual period. But fourteen days falls in the middle of this interval and is usually applied as an average for identifying ovulation.

THE DAYS OF A 28-DAY CYCLE
WHEN SEXUAL INTERCOURSE
MAY LEAD TO PREGNANCY

NOVEMBER

	1●	2●	3●	4●	5●	6
7	8	9	10	11	⑫♂	⑬♂
⑭♀	⑮♀	16	17	18	19	20
21	22	23	24	25	26	27
28	29●	30●				

♀ The twenty-four hour ovum survival period which may cover parts of two days

● (menstrual flow)

♂ 2-day sperm survival period

Consider the calendar of a woman who has a regular twenty-eight-day cycle.

If, as the calendar illustrates, she begins one menstrual period on November 1 and the next on November 29, she could count back about fourteen days from the last day of her cycle, Sunday the twenty-eighth, and estimate that ovulation occurred Sunday the fourteenth or Monday the fifteenth. She would know that the egg could survive for a maximum of twenty-four hours, which could cover parts of the fourteenth and fifteenth. And she would know that sperm deposited in her body on Friday night, the twelfth, or Saturday night, the thirteenth, might be still alive and well enough to fertilize that egg. For this woman, the possible pregnancy days are November 12–15.

You undoubtedly have some questions about the timing of ovulation and the means of predicting it. First of all, you may be wondering, if a woman has a cycle that is longer or shorter than twenty-eight days, when would ovulation occur then? The general rule here is that no matter how long the cycle is, ovulation still occurs about fourteen days before the menstrual period begins. In a twenty-eight-day cycle, then, ovulation occurs in the middle of the cycle. But the "midcycle ovulation" observation does *not* always apply. For instance, if a woman has a thirty-five day cycle, she would probably ovulate about day twenty-one. And that is *not* the middle of the cycle. Similarly if she has a twenty-four-day cycle, ovulation would take place around day ten. Again, that is not the middle of the cycle.

Second, you will notice that we have been discussing "backward" information, that is, by counting back fourteen or so days to identify when ovulation probably occurred. But married couples are often interested in *predicting* when ovulation *will* occur. Unfortunately for them, they have to settle for the backward approach and hope that the timing of menstrual cycle events is about the same from month to month. There are some other means married couples used to pinpoint the "possible pregnancy period," that is, a woman's *fertile period*. And since someday this information may be of practical interest to you, you should know about these techniques. But you will have to wait until Chapter 6 for that.

Third, it may have occurred to you that, with such a relatively short fertile period, it is surprising that so many women become pregnant. Actually, however, three or four days can be longer than you might think. For instance, consider the woman with a twenty-eight-day cycle. She might not have sexual intercourse with her husband during her menstrual flow (although if they did have intercourse then, it would not be harmful to either of them). That would mean that she might have intercourse during the twenty-three days of the cycle that are left. As we have calculated above, intercourse on four of those twenty-three days could lead to pregnancy.

Let's say she didn't have any idea when those four days might appear. (A recent national survey of American teenage girls indicated that most of them *didn't* know when the egg was released. Over a third of them inaccurately believed that a woman was most likely to become pregnant "right before, during, or after her period.") If she then had intercourse just once a week at regular intervals throughout the cycle, she would almost surely have sperm deposited in her body during the fertile period. Even if she *did* know all the facts about the timing of ovulation and the survival period for sperm, her cycle might end up being shorter or longer than she expected, and thus, she might have sexual intercourse on, or within two days before, the day the egg was released.

The Sperm's Journey

Let's return to the point at which the sperm are still in the man's body. You know that the man must have an erection and then eventually, an ejaculation, before sperm can be released in significant quantities. We say "in significant quantities" because some sperm may be included in the secretions that are released in small quantities from the penis before the orgasm occurs. If these sperm enter a woman's body, they too are capable of uniting with the female's egg.

Thus, how do the sperm make their way into a woman's fallopian tube? The most obvious answer is "through sexual intercourse." But this is just the primary way. Sometimes when a man and woman are having difficulty in achieving a pregnancy, a doctor will take some of the husband's semen or the semen from another man (or a combination of the husband's and another man's semen) and

TRAVELS OF THE SPERM TOWARD THE EGG

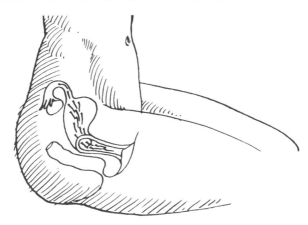

introduce it by artificial means into the woman's cervix and uterus. This is *artificial insemination,* a process which has proven to be very useful in cases where a man does not have a sufficient number of his own sperm—or where the chemicals in a woman's vagina are so hostile to his sperm that they have trouble reaching the cervix and uterus (this happens only occasionally).

But the main way sperm are introduced is through sexual intercourse. In the course of ejaculation, millions of sperm enter the woman's body. Doctors have found that at least sixty million sperm per cubic centimeter of semen are necessary to ensure that conception at least has a chance to occur, although usually four to five times that many enter the vagina.

Why Are There So *Many* Sperm?

You might be surprised that so many sperm are released, since only one ever enters the egg and joins with its nucleus. But this huge number of sperm is necessary.

First, the reception given the sperm in the vagina is often very hostile. A woman's vagina has many secretions that keep it clean and lubricated. Unfortunately for the sperm, these secretions are very acidic and a number of sperm die right there. Even though the sperm have some ability to resist the acidic surroundings, not all of them survive. As a matter of fact, the number of sperm that survive is reduced dramatically. Of the 66 to 867 million sperm deposited during sexual intercourse, fewer than 100 of them are present in the fallopian tubes at the time an egg and sperm join forces. This represents a reduction of about 99.99 percent! The largest number of sperm are lost in the vagina, where they simply die and disintegrate. But further, of those that do get into the uterus (where the environment is much more alkaline, the opposite of acidic, and hence more receptive for sperm), about half are "lost" because they enter the wrong fallopian tube. You recall that there is usually an egg present in just one tube at a time.

Second, such a large number of sperm are deposited during sexual intercourse because although only one enters the egg, the cooperation of a number of sperm is necessary to break down the protective wall of the female cell. Sperm carry a special "breaking and entering" fluid, an enzyme technically known as *hyaluronidase*, which has the capacity to break down the membrane that surrounds the yolk and nucleus of the egg. Chemical contributions from more than one sperm are necessary before the chosen one can enter. It's like a team effort.

The Uphill Struggle

But let's turn back to the topic of the sperm's journey. During intercourse they are deposited in the vagina, usually very near the cervix. If something is blocking the cervix, they will not go any farther than this. During most of a woman's cycle, this indeed is what happens. Until recently, it was thought that sperm that were introduced at any time of a woman's menstrual cycle would begin to make the upward journey toward her tubes—even if no egg was present. But now it is clear that a woman's cervix has a special type of natural chemical barrier that keeps out sperm during those portions of the cycle when pregnancy is unlikely to occur. Most of the time the cervical secretions are thick and sticky, and sperm just cannot penetrate them. But as ovulation approaches, these secretions become clear and watery, and thus the barrier disappears.

If the timing is right (or wrong, depending on a couple's point of view), sperm swim up through the cervix, into the uterus and eventually into the fallopian tubes. And this is quite a journey for those tiny cells. It's uphill all the way. The ability of sperm to defy gravity and make the ascent into the woman's pelvic region is explained by three factors.

First, during ejaculation, sperm are released in spurts from the urethra inside the penis. These spurts give the sperm a push in the direction they want to go. Second, as you have already read, the sperm have an impressive capacity for self-movement. They start whipping their tails right away, and with every lashing movement, they move farther up the female's reproductive tract. Third, it appears that a certain chemical in semen *(prostaglandin)* has a definite reaction on the woman's uterus. It actually causes the uterus to contract in and out and sperm are effectively sucked into it and toward the tubes.

Fertilization—the Merging of the Egg and Sperm

If the sperm are deposited in the uterus and if there is an ovum available in the fallopian tube (or one arrives within forty-eight hours), there is a good possibility that fertilization will occur. But how do the egg and sperm go about joining forces?

A large number of sperm rush to the egg, each one of them competing for it, and all of them releasing that special breaking-and-entering fluid, hyaluronidase. All of a sudden, one sperm succeeds in entering the egg. Then two important things happen. The head of that chosen sperm, that is, its nucleus, merges with the nucleus of the egg and forms one cell. (You recall that the egg and sperm alone are just "half cells," that is, they contain only twenty-three chromosomes each. When they merge, however, the newly formed cell has all of the forty-six chromosomes of a regular cell, half of which are donated by the mother, half by the father.) Second, after this fertilization occurs, the new cell responds chemically to prevent any other sperm from entering.

WHAT IS THE NEW BABY'S SEX?

In the first chapter, we explained that you are a male because the sperm that fertilized your mother's egg carried a Y sex chromosome rather than an X sex chromosome. But exactly how is this important matter determined?

The answer to this question is not exactly clear. We are still putting together parts of the sex-determination puzzle. And the desire to work out a solution to this puzzle is nothing new. People for generations have been working on this question, and over the years have managed to produce an incredible number of "explanations"—all of which have been wrong!

Some early scientists claimed that the stronger of the two partners would determine the sex of the child. If, for instance, the wife was very aggressive, the child would be a girl. (Other observers felt that just the opposite would occur with aggressive wives giving birth to more males.) Still others maintained that a mother's diet was the key influence on the sex of unborn children. Since everyone knew that girls were made of sugar and spice, ladies wanting sons were warned to avoid sweets and candy and advised to eat good "masculine" foods—like rich red meat!

Ancient Greek doctors explained to their patients that boys were made in the right side of the body, girls in the left (they thought the right side of the body was stronger, and thus likely to yield what they felt was the stronger of the two sexes). On the basis of this advice, men seeking sons actually would tie up their left testicles hoping that sperm would be released from only their right-sided sex organs! Similarly, they would lie on their right side during intercourse—and try to position themselves so that the pregnancy would begin in what they thought was the right-handed chamber of their wife's uterus!

You might think this right-left theory is really absurd (and it is!), but it had a great deal of support even into this century. A respected English doctor in the 1920s claimed that he had solved the whole sex-determination riddle by discovering that "boy eggs" were released from a woman's right ovary, "girl eggs" from her left. He told his patients that, while they could not plan the sex of their first child, they could do so with all subsequent children as long as they kept in mind the month of conception and sex of their first born. Assuming that the ovaries alternated between boy and girl months, they were advised to keep careful records after that and plan later pregnancies accordingly.

Despite these efforts to control their babies' sex, couples continued to have the same sex ratio we have today: about 106 male babies born for every 100 female babies. It is curious why there is the constant (although slight) excess of male babies at birth. What is even *more* curious is the theory that there may be up to 160 male conceptions for every 100 female conceptions. For some reason male fetuses do not seem to survive as well during pregnancy as do female fetuses. However, the greater number of original male fetuses favors a more equal sex ratio at birth.

Today many different types of scientists are looking into the question of human sex preselection. Sociologists, for instance, are studying certain populations and time periods where the sex ratio (that is, the proportion of males to females at the time of birth) is unusually high or low. It's been shown, for instance, that during and right after major wars, more male babies than usual are born.

Similarly, it has been documented that young women—and those who have never had a baby before—are more likely to have a male baby than are older women and those who are already mothers. And medical researchers are examining the types of biological factors that might affect the sex of a child. Some doctors now believe that the acidity or alkalinity of a woman's vagina may be important, with high acidity reducing the chances of survival of the male sperm. Women who follow this theory may wash their vagina out with a baking soda and water preparation to reduce acidity. Additionally, some physicians now believe that the timing of sexual intercourse within the menstrual cycle is important in determining the baby's sex. They may advise a woman who wants a son to have intercourse early in her fertile period, and the ones desiring a daughter to have intercourse somewhat later, as close to ovulation as possible.

We still have a great deal to learn about the factors that determine which sperm—the X or Y variety—enters a female egg. But when we do get the answer, imagine what an effect it will have! Parents would know exactly what gender of baby was on the way—and they could have a name and wardrobe all chosen. But more important, they would truly be able to plan their families, having only the number of children they want.

Think of all the large families you know. Chances are that in many of them the older children are of the same sex. Perhaps their parents tried "just one more time" to have a baby of the opposite sex to round out their family. Maybe if they had a means of choosing their offspring's gender in advance, they would have had fewer children. And if all parents had this information—and had fewer children—this could be very important in reducing the problems caused by an exploding population. This appears to be particularly true in countries such as India, where there is a strong preference for male children, and couples keep having babies until they have all the sons they want.

TWINS, TRIPLETS—OR MORE?

In the great majority of cases, women have just one baby at a time. This is because there is usually just one egg released from the ovary each cycle, which, if fertilized by a sperm, develops into a single child. Occasionally, however, more than one baby may develop in a woman's uterus at the same time.

The most common type of multiple birth is twinning. You probably know of at least one set of twins in your school. About one in every eighty births involves twins. But you have probably noticed that not all twins look alike. This is because there are two distinct types of twinning, *fraternal twinning* and *identical twinning.*

If a woman's ovaries work overtime during one menstrual cycle and release more than one egg, it is possible that more than one egg will join up with a sperm. When more than one such union occurs, the resulting babies may not look alike, and indeed one may be a boy, the other a girl. This is fraternal twinning, and both children develop independently from different sperm and egg unions.

When, however, only one of a woman's eggs is fertilized, and soon after splits into two separate parts, each containing exactly the same types of chromosomal materials, the result is identical twins. These are look-alike children who have the exact same genetic makeup and share equally in the contributions of their mother and father.

As was the case with sex determination, we still have a great deal to learn about twinning. We know now that the older a woman is and the more babies she has had, the greater are her chances of having twins. We also know that fraternal twinning is affected by heredity. If a woman's mother or grandmother had fraternal twins, she is more likely to have fraternal twins than is a girl whose family has no history of fraternal twinning (twinning does not "skip generations," as it was once thought). There is no type of hereditary influence operating in the birth of identical twins.

Only rarely do we read about the birth of triplets (about one in every 10,000 births) or quadruplets (about one in every 500,000 births). When you next read a story about a woman giving birth to four or even five babies at the same time, it may be that she was taking one of the so-called fertility drugs. If a woman is having trouble becoming pregnant, and her doctor thinks that her problem is that she is not releasing eggs from her ovaries, he may try to stimulate ovulation by giving her medicine. Sometimes this medicine goes beyond the call of duty and not one but a number of eggs are released, presenting the possibility of multiple fertilization.

But fertilization is just the beginning. A new life (or maybe more than one) has been created and for the next nine or so months, a fantastic rate of growth will take place.

chapter 5

Beyond Conception

AFTER FERTILIZATION, THEN WHAT?

Just a few hours after a sperm (with the help of other sperm) has managed to penetrate the protective wall of the egg and the nucleus of the sperm and egg have merged, the new cell begins to grow by a process of cell division, or *cleavage*.

The fertilized egg cell divides into two cells, then four, then eight, and so forth. While this cell division is occurring, the fertilized egg does not just stay in the fallopian tube. It continues its journey down the tube toward the uterus, being well nourished in its travels by the chemicals the egg carries with it—and by some of the fluids it finds in the walls of the fallopian tubes.

About four days after it is fertilized, the egg enters the uterus. By this time it has grown significantly and is a ball-shaped cluster of rapidly dividing cells. If you were to look at the egg using a microscope, you would see that it looked very much like a mulberry.

The mass of cells, after arriving in the uterus, remains another day or two and then begins the process known as *implantation*, a process in which it embeds itself into the wall of the well-prepared uterus, drawing nourishment from the richly supplied tissues.

The timing of implantation is very important. The lining of the uterus has to be "just right" if the pregnancy is to continue normally. If, for example, the egg has moved too rapidly down the tube—or if it did not remain the extra day or two after it arrived in the uterus—the endometrial lining would not be ready to receive it. If the egg has not developed the way it should have during its trip in the tubes, it will not be mature enough to go through the implantation process.

By the time the fertilized egg, now know as an *embryo*, begins to embed itself into the endometrium, it contains as many as one hundred individual cells, some of which have begun to take on specific functions. One portion of this embryo, for instance, is useful in breaking through a few layers of the woman's uterine tissue. The endometrium promotes these burrowing attempts by closing up the broken tissues so that it almost completely conceals the embryo.

If you were able to take a look at the uterus right now, you would see only a slight bump on its lining, but inside that "bump" all types of things are happening.

One of those important happenings is the secretion of a specialized chemical that "announces" the pregnancy to the woman's body. This chemical is *human chorionic gonadotropic hormone*, abbreviated *HCG*. This pregnancy-signal hormone has a dramatic effect on the direction a woman's menstrual cycle takes. In effect, it stops the regular cycle.

As we pointed out in Chapter 3, in most cycles, when no fertilized egg appears, the high levels of estrogen and progesterone signal the woman's master gland to stop producing LH. Without LH, the follicle in which the egg grew, the so-called yellow body, can no longer secrete the estrogen and progesterone so necessary to maintain the blood and tissue lining of the uterus. And so the endometrium is released from the body. But when the egg *does* meet and join up with a sperm, the events are very different. That uterine lining is *very* much needed.

The embryo sends HCG into the bloodstream (about a week or so after the fertilization occurs) and HCG has an immediate effect on the yellow body. Instead of disintegrating, as it would in a regular menstrual cycle, the yellow body is further stimulated and begins to produce increasing amounts of estrogen and progesterone. These hormones ensure that the lining of the uterus develops even further.

With high levels of these hormones dominating a woman's body, she has no menstrual flow. Often this failure to menstruate is her first signal that she is going to have a baby.

To confirm a pregnancy, however, she will probably go to the doctor and have a type of urine test that can detect the presence of HCG. HCG does not appear in a level high enough for detection in a pregnant woman's urine until a few weeks after it is first released. But eventually it can be found and its presence—along with a number of other physical signs of pregnancy—enables a doctor to make a definite diagnosis.

WHAT HAPPENS DURING PREGNANCY?

You probably already know that a human pregnancy lasts "about nine months." But to be more specific, since different months have different lengths, you should be aware that, on the average, a pregnancy lasts about 266 days, counting from the day of fertilization to the day of birth. Some doctors prefer to start the pregnancy

HUMAN EMBRYO—6TH WEEK OF PREGNANCY (ACTUAL SIZE)

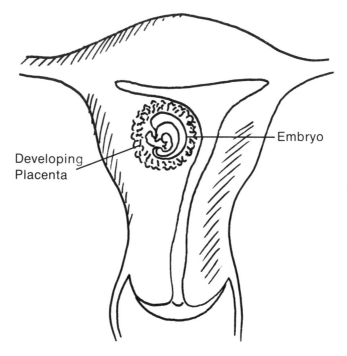

countdown on the date of the woman's last menstrual period because this is a definite single date (as opposed to the incidences of sexual intercourse that may have occurred on more than one day during the fertile period). Counting from the date of the last menstrual period, the pregnancy interval is about 280 days.

The First Three Months

Pregnancy is usually described in terms of three separate three-month intervals, or *trimesters*. The 280-day period is also divided into the period of the *embryo* (approximately the first eight weeks) and the period of the *fetus* (approximately the last thirty-two weeks).

During the first weeks in the uterus, the basic human organs and systems are formed, and the new life is very fragile and delicate. The organ that eventually becomes a full-fledged heart begins to function and the embryo's head, eye sockets, ear membranes, and even the beginnings of arms and legs become visible (that is, if you could look inside the uterus). By the end of the first two months of pregnancy, the embryo is a fairly complete organism, even though it is only about an inch long.

Also during these early weeks, the *placenta* develops. Made up of cells contributed partly by the embryo and partly by the mother, the placenta is attached to the uterine wall and permits the bloodstreams of the mother and baby to be very close to each other without ever becoming mixed. In a very efficient manner, the placenta, which is connected to the fetus by the *umbilical cord,*

HUMAN EMBRYO—10TH WEEK OF PREGNANCY (ACTUAL SIZE)

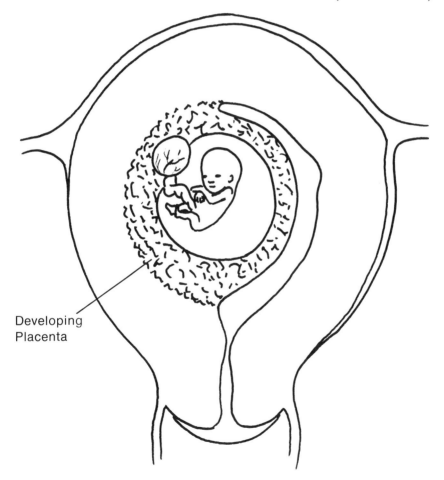

Developing
Placenta

allows oxygen and nutrients to pass from the mother to the child, and waste products to pass in the reverse direction from the embryo into the bloodstream of the mother.

Additionally, the placenta acts as a storage area for food, iron, and proteins, all of which the embryo will need in later stages of growth, and it allows the mother to share her chemical defenses against diseases with the new baby she is carrying.

The Second Three Months

During this midtrimester of pregnancy, both the woman and her doctor begin to notice very dramatic signs that a new life has begun.

By about the twentieth week of pregnancy, the doctor examining the woman (usually a particular type of doctor known as an *obstetrician*) can hear the fetal heartbeat very clearly. About the same time, the mother can feel the movement of the baby as its arms and legs are moved around (this is the time of *quickening*). At the beginning she may just feel a slight flutter, but later, the growing baby leaves no doubt in her mind about the fact that it is getting bigger and stronger and wants the world to know about it.

During this second trimester, when the baby is technically known as a fetus, the male or female sex organs begin to develop rapidly. You know the determination of sex is made at the moment of conception, but it takes some time for these reproductive organs to distinguish themselves. Also, about this time, the growing baby's eyes are formed and it even becomes sensitive to light. Similarly, its hearing apparatus develops so significantly that it becomes sensitive to the sounds around it. During this time, and for most of the pregnancy, the baby is completely surrounded by fluid and simply free-floats in what sometimes is called the "bag of waters," and it is not terribly disturbed by the mother's movements, or even by any jolts her body may receive.

The Last Three Months

As you can see from the pictures on page 64 and 65, the normal position the fetus assumes is an upside-down one, with the baby's head facing the woman's cervix and vagina. The uterus has expanded in this time period—but the real expansion, both of the uterus and the fetus itself, is yet to come.

14TH WEEK OF PREGNANCY (ACTUAL SIZE)

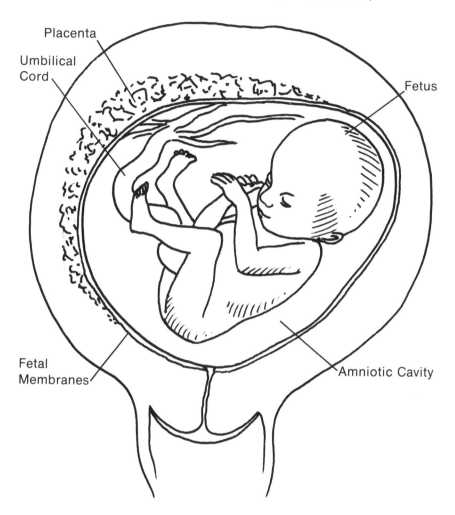

In the last trimester of pregnancy, just before the birth, there is a tremendous increase in the size of the fetus. About half of its total weight is added in these last three months. And it goes without saying that the prospective mother is going to show some definite effects. While through the first two trimesters of pregnancy she had some slight swelling in her abdomen, and probably wore some loose maternity clothes, it was in the last months that she really "looked pregnant." Her uterus had expanded to about five hundred times its original size, and her breasts became sig-

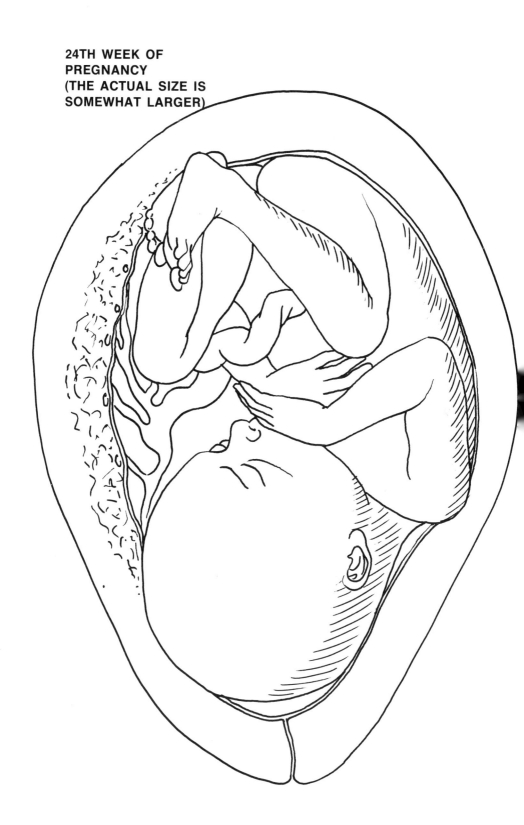

24TH WEEK OF
PREGNANCY
(THE ACTUAL SIZE IS
SOMEWHAT LARGER)

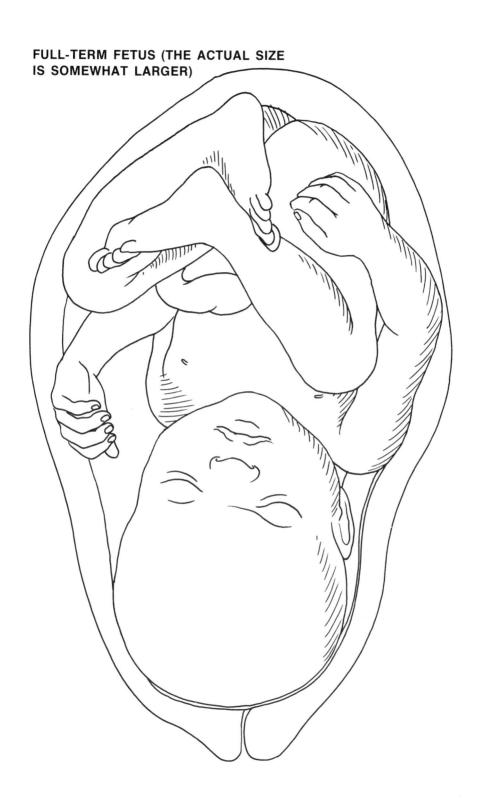

FULL-TERM FETUS (THE ACTUAL SIZE IS SOMEWHAT LARGER)

nificantly larger. Not only was she carrying inside her a baby who would likely weigh around six to eight pounds when it was born, but she also had to accommodate the placenta, umbilical cord, and bag of waters. And not only was her pelvic area changing in pregnancy, but the mammary glands in her breasts were changing in a way that would allow them to function after the birth.

THE PREGNANCY IS OVER AND A BABY IS BORN

During most of the pregnancy period, the uterus is very relaxed and the growing baby comfortably resides in the uterus. The presence of the hormone progesterone is particularly helpful in ensuring that the uterus temporarily avoids its natural contractions.

But near the end of the pregnancy, the once-calm uterus begins to act up. The master gland sends out a special type of hormone that has a stimulating effect on the uterus, and the placenta begins to secrete decreasing amounts of progesterone. The effect is that the uterus begins to contract, and the *first phase of labor* begins. This is a phase during which the female's body prepares for the birth of the child. The phase may last twelve or so hours in women who have never had a baby before, or about eight hours in women who are already mothers.

What is known by doctors as the *second phase of labor* is what you would actually call the birth itself, when the baby passes through the cervix and vagina into the outside world. Often a doctor will make this phase easier by making a slight cut in the entrance of the mother's vagina to prevent unnecessary stretching of her tissues. (This procedure is known as an *episiotomy.*) The *third phase of labor* begins after the child is born and involves the expulsion of the placenta and other fetal membranes (known together as the "afterbirth"). These structures have performed their function and are no longer needed inside the woman's body.

A NATURAL FOOD SUPPLY

All during the course of the pregnancy, the mother's breasts were preparing in a way that would allow them to offer a perfect type of food, as well as additional forms of immunity against disease, to a hungry, newborn infant. When the infant is born, her breasts change even more dramatically and become noticeably enlarged and full. The mammary glands have become larger and the ducts of the breasts are prepared to release milk. This release of milk from the breast is called *lactation* (also known as breast-feeding and nursing).

Some women choose to take advantage of this natural milk supply. If they do, their milk will be released by the suckling action of the infant when it is brought to the breast. But other mothers choose not to nurse, and feed their babies a specially designed formula that is very much like a mother's own milk. In this case, there is no suckling action on their nipples, and the milk production stops within a few days. Breast-feeding—like so many other aspects of life—is a matter of choice.

WHERE DOES THE MAN FIT INTO ALL OF THIS?

After reading these last two chapters you may have concluded that pregnancy and childbirth are strictly "female matters." From the time when the sperm and the egg united to form a new life, we made no further reference to the male and focused on the events that take place within the woman's body. But a pregnancy has an impact on the man as well as the woman. And some researchers think that they have evidence that the impact can be *physical* as well as psychological.

Most studies indicate that a husband, when he first hears that he is going to become a father, immediately feels a new—and very sobering—sense of responsibility. The growing baby, who came into existence after one of his sperm cells had fertilized his wife's egg, is going to depend on *him* for food, clothing, education—and a great deal of love and emotional support.

You probably already know that many women have some slight discomfort, and possibly "morning sickness," especially during the early part of their pregnancy. But did you know that some expectant fathers do, too? Extensive anthropological studies in New Guinea and East Africa have reported that a significant number of men experience morning sickness, feel very thirsty or hungry, and occasionally report that they can "feel the growth of something inside them!" Similar studies of American fathers-to-be have also reported nausea, vomiting, faintness, loss of appetite, and leg cramps. Perhaps these men are having a type of sympathetic reaction to their wife's symptoms, or perhaps this is their psychological reaction to the impending birth—and the natural anxiety that they may have about meeting all the responsibilities that go with being a parent.

THE MIRACLE OF LIFE

In our age of medical sophistication, it is easy to forget for a moment that the process of human life is a very intricate and delicate one, one over which we often have little control. If just one of the hundreds of reproductive events goes wrong, there may be no baby at all. The ability to become a parent cannot just be taken for granted. Many things can—and sometimes do—go wrong. Therefore, it will be useful to review briefly some of the major events that must occur before a new life is brought into the world. And we should also give some consideration to some of the events that *don't* have to occur.

We started our whole discussion of the reproductive process with the sperm and the egg. Before a pregnancy is possible, these cells must both be healthy and fully developed—and they must be on the type of "reproductive timetable" that allows them to get together in the first place.

If a man does not have enough sperm (remember, he needs quite a few of them before he can become a father), or if a woman is not releasing eggs, pregnancy cannot occur. Next, the sperm must have the opportunity to enter the female body and make the trip to her fallopian tubes. That is, the sperm must be released into her body during ejaculation (although some may escape before ejaculation) and these cells must survive the sometimes very inhospitable greeting they receive in the vagina.

So male ejaculation (or some type of insemination) must occur before pregnancy becomes possible. But what about a woman? Does she ejaculate something and have an orgasm? Is it necessary for her to have an orgasm before pregnancy can occur?

A woman does *not* secrete any substance that is comparable to semen. Her sexual secretions come primarily from those glands within her vagina that serve to lubricate her body in case intercourse is to take place. But a woman *can* have an orgasm that brings about the same type of pleasurable body sensations as does a man's orgasm. Her orgasm, or climax, may occur after her clitoris, the pea-shaped organ above her urethra, becomes stimulated. This can happen in a number of ways. In intercourse the penis may come in contact with the clitoris, causing it to become enlarged and engorged with blood. Similarly, this may happen during the type of sexual "foreplay" that precedes intercourse. Also, a woman can stimulate her own clitoris, that is, she can masturbate, often to the point of orgasm.

A woman's orgasm, however, is *not* necessary for pregnancy to occur. There are some doctors who feel that female orgasm can make the vagina and cervical areas less acid (therefore, more alkaline), and thus may have an effect of favoring the male-producing sperm over the female-producing sperm. But this theory is not yet confirmed. What is important here, is that female orgasm does not affect the probability of conception.

If the egg and sperm do get together and form one cell, the new life must survive the trip down the fallopian tube so that it can become implanted in the uterus. If something goes wrong there, for instance, if the embryo begins to become implanted in the fallopian tube (or somewhere else) before it gets to the uterus, the pregnancy cannot continue. (This is what is known as an *ectopic pregnancy*, a situation that must be corrected by surgery as soon as it is diagnosed.)

When it does enter the uterus, the endometrium must be "just so" before the implantation process can be successful. If estrogen and progesterone have not worked perfectly, the pregnancy will not continue. During the nine-month stay in the uterus, the growing babies need to have all their baby membranes in perfect operating order—and they need a balanced diet (something for which they are completely dependent on their mothers).

So human reproduction is complicated, and becoming a parent is not always as easy as couples assume it is going to be. Surveys have shown that about 10 percent of couples are unable to have children, that is, they are *sterile*. Some couples wait for many months or years before a pregnancy begins. Others find that although the wife becomes pregnant, she loses the baby early in pregnancy—that is, she has a *miscarriage*. These couples usually seek help from an understanding obstetrician, and they are more successful in later attempts.

With all the possible things that can go wrong, it is amazing that we have nearly four billion people in the world right now—all of whom survived the chancy events related to conception, pregnancy, and birth. And the population continues to grow. Some people today want to have as many children as they physically can. But more and more couples are deciding to limit their family size. They may decide to have four children, or no children. But at least they plan. And in order to assure that they have only the number of children they can afford (emotionally as well as financially), they turn to one of the many available means of family planning we have today.

You've probably heard about many of these means of birth control, and perhaps you've read about some of the newer ones in newspapers and magazines. But you should have some of the details about what they are and how they prevent births, because when you are married, you too will probably want to plan when (if at all) babies will come into your life.

chapter 6

Birth Control: Past, Present, and Future

ON THE TIMING, SPACING, AND PREVENTION OF BABIES

Recent advances in the science of human reproduction have had some very practical implications. First, medical researchers now have a better understanding than before of some of the factors that cause infertility (that is, difficulty in having a baby), and they have been able to develop a wide variety of techniques to correct some of these problems. Second, scientists now have the facts that allow them to develop means of *interfering* with the normal progression of reproductive events. With these methods, a husband and wife can not only plan the size of their family, but also can have better control over the timing of pregnancy.

Spider Eggs and Cat Livers

Living in our modern world and reading about the so-called "contraception revolution," it is easy to assume that birth control is a new subject, one that was not studied until well into the twentieth century. But this is not true. Egyptian medical documents, written almost four thousand years ago, indicate that couples in earliest recorded history saw the advantage of freeing themselves from the burden of childbearing each and every year. Children were wanted, of course, but not in unlimited quantities! And it was not just individual couples then who saw the benefits of controlling the number of children they had. Aristotle (384–322 B.C.), the ancient Greek philosopher, was one of the first scientific observers to point out that limited human expansion was in everybody's best interest. He proposed a type of "zero population growth" for the city-states of Greece.

But despite the serious intentions of earlier people to plan their families and avoid unwanted babies, they were not very successful. The first problem was that many of them just did not understand how a pregnancy came about. Intercourse occurred one day and a baby appeared about nine months later; it was not easy to see the link between these two events.

Those who came up with the hypothesis that sexual intercourse led to babies met some pretty convincing contrary arguments; when very young girls or older women had sexual intercourse, no babies appeared. And some fully mature young women with active sex lives never produced children. How was this explained?

The primary "explanation" was that pregnancy and childbirth were mysterious female functions that occurred spontaneously in most, but not all, women. The man, according to this theory, had no involvement whatsoever in the creation of new life. An expectant father often thought that his wife must have eaten a type of food that made her pregnant, or had come under the influence of the sun or the moon—or maybe the pregnancy and birth "just happened," as menstrual bleeding seemed to do.

Operating on the assumption that it was just the wife who played a role in human reproduction, early efforts to postpone or avoid pregnancy focused exclusively on the woman. A lady's private physician suggested that she sip carefully blended baby-proof teas, snack on spider's eggs, or eat honey containing the bodies of dead bees. Some other well-meaning advisers suggested that women wear charms to avoid pregnancy. In ancient Rome and Greece, women often wore jewelry made from the uterus of a lioness, the tooth of a child, or the liver from a female cat. Needless to say, if a woman ever managed to survive the side effects of these "tried and true" birth-control methods, she probably would have a child about nine months later. It was at this point that she had the option of implementing the most widespread and effective form of birth control: If the child was not wanted, or if it was of the "wrong" sex, it would be killed within a few days of birth. In early societies this practice, known as *infanticide*, was one of the most widely used forms of population limitation.

Birds and Bees—and Sneezing

Significant progress in the area of birth control was not made until the male role in reproduction was suspected. But even then, the problem was confused by a massive amount of misinformation.

It is not known who first observed that it takes two to make a baby. Aristotle must have had some clue as to what was going on when he suggested that babies resulted from the combination of menstrual blood and male semen. It all seemed very logical to him. Since pregnant women did not have menstrual periods, the blood must just stay inside of them and turn into a baby. According to

Aristotle, the male's "seed" was essential in providing the material for the growing child's soul and brain.

When scientific methods became more sophisticated, and the male sex cell was identified in semen, it was suggested that each sperm contained all the human parts. Drawings made during the seventeenth century of the sperm showed them to be an "infinity of animals like tadpoles," each with tiny arms and legs. Indeed, sperm were viewed as being complete miniature human beings, which had to be introduced into the woman's body so they could grow. (This theory was "confirmed" when other eager scientists claimed that when they looked at the semen of other animals, they saw horses, donkeys, or whatever the relevant species was!)

Confusing—and inaccurate—as these sperm theories were, they did suggest that pregnancy could be avoided if sperm could be kept out of the female's body. Thus, one well-meaning physician advised his female patients to "rise roughly, sneeze and blow your nose several times and call out in a loud voice" after sexual intercourse. To further improve her chances of expelling sperm she could also jump violently backward eight to nine times or simply jump up and down for a few minutes. Additionally, she may have been told to hold her breath during her husband's orgasm so that her next exhaled breath would "push the sperm out."

Obviously, these methods were not very effective and women continued to have unwanted children. But not *all* early birth-control experiments were this unsuccessful. Indeed, as will be pointed out throughout this chapter, many of our current "modern" means can be traced back hundreds and even thousands of years. But in our case, these methods of controlling conception, instead of being derived from a mixture of superstition and semiscientific experimentation, are based on a firm understanding of human reproduction and the mechanisms for controlling it.

BIRTH CONTROL TODAY

Only fifty or sixty years ago, when scientists were perfecting some new and very sophisticated approaches to human fertility control, there was a widespread belief that contraception was immoral—and even sinful. Some of the early birth-control pioneers in the United States (such as a nurse named Margaret Sanger) were actually jailed for distributing information about family planning. But this has changed. Indeed, this is what the contraception revolution is all about.

Not only do married couples now have a wide variety of highly effective methods from which to choose, but the idea of contraception and birth planning has become acceptable to most all individuals. (Ninety-seven percent of young married American couples have used or intend to use some form of birth control.) All the major religions of the world have approved a couple's right to limit the size of their families (although in some religions the followers are told *which* methods they can and cannot use). Most countries in the world have changed those laws that made access to birth control so difficult years ago, and the majority of them are actually setting up clinics that encourage married people to use some type of birth control. Around the world, millions of couples have decided that their lives, and those of their children, will be more fulfilled if they have only the number of sons and daughters they can economically and emotionally afford.

MAY THE EGG AND SPERM NEVER MEET

Most of our modern means of birth control attempt to prevent the egg and sperm from ever getting together in the first place. Our current efforts to keep these two cells away from each other fall into four general categories:

1. Those methods that prevent the release of the egg from the ovary, or prevent its trip down the fallopian tube (oral contraceptives, birth-control shots, and female sterilization).
2. Those that keep the sperm from entering the woman's vagina (withdrawal, condom, and vasectomy).
3. Those that keep sperm from entering the body *only* during the time when conception is most likely to occur (calendar and temperature rhythm).
4. Those that allow sperm into the vagina, but prevent them from getting into the uterus and fallopian tubes (diaphragm, spermicides, and the mini-pill).

There's another method of birth control (the intrauterine device), which cannot be included in the above groups, because it does not necessarily act to keep the egg and the sperm apart. Its mechanism of action is in a class by itself—a class that can only be described as "unknown." But we'll get back to this mystery method of birth control in a later section. Let's first take a look at each of the four ways the meeting of the sperm and the egg is nipped in the bud.

STOPPING OR BLOCKING THE EGG

Oral Contraceptives ("The Pill")

The idea of taking some type of medicine to prevent pregnancy is nothing new. The Talmud, the ancient book of Jewish law, states that "a woman is allowed to drink a cup of roots in order to become sterile." Sources throughout history have referred to weird potions of roots, weeds, honey, and even froth from a camel's mouth as means of preventing pregnancy. The Bible tells of the wives of Jacob, Leah and Rachel, who used the root of the mandrake plant with a similar goal in mind. This example is particularly interesting, because it is the product of a similar plant, the Mexican yam, which provided the raw materials for the first versions of our current "birth-control medicine."

There are a number of different pills or tablets that are used by women to prevent pregnancy, but the ones we are discussing here have earned the title "The Pill," because they are so effective and so widely used. The primary way The Pill prevents pregnancy is by changing the levels of hormones in a woman's body and thereby interrupting the cycle of events that normally would lead to the release of an egg from one of her ovaries.

You may remember from Chapter 3 that a woman's body has a built-in thermostat system, which regulates the release of her hormones. When the level of one hormone is very low, another is released. When the levels of certain hormones are very high, a different hormone is sent out through the bloodstream.

During the menstrual flow, the levels of both estrogen and progesterone are very low. In response to the relative lack of these basic hormones, the woman's master glands sends out FSH (follicle-stimulating hormone) to get things going again. FSH acts on her ovaries and causes the egg cells to develop and the follicles to begin secreting increasing amounts of estrogen.

When estrogen levels get high, the master gland sends out

another hormone, LH, which helps trigger ovulation. After ovulation, the ovarian follicle secretes progesterone—and when the level of this hormone is sufficiently high, the master gland gets back into action, this time recalling LH. Progesterone and estrogen secretion cannot keep going on without LH, so levels fall. The menstrual flow begins and the woman is back again at the beginning of her cycle.

The complex interaction between the ovarian hormones and the pituitary or master gland, which is summarized so simply above, was difficult to figure out. It took many years of research to understand. But something additional derived from all this research was a way of controlling that complex hormonal interaction. That's where The Pill comes in.

The most common type of Pill is the "combined" type, that is, it contains both estrogen and progesterone in every tablet. A woman taking these two hormones throughout her cycle keeps her hormone levels high. If progesterone and estrogen are present in sufficient quantities, there's no signal to the pituitary to send out FSH. Without FSH, no egg in the ovary begins to develop. Without an egg, there's no ovulation. Without ovulation, there's no chance for conception.

The Pill has a few backup capacities that result in pregnancy prevention just in case an egg does manage to grow in the ovary and be released into the fallopian tube. For instance, the oral contraceptives may change the nature of the chemicals within a woman's vagina and in the area of her cervix in such a way that sperm do not get a chance to start their journey to the fallopian tubes. The Pill also may change the conditions in the uterus so that the reception the fertilized egg gets there is less than ideal so that it cannot implant itself in the lining. But the primary action of The Pill is ovulation prevention.

To be effective, the oral contraceptives must be taken according to schedule. Women who forget one pill are advised to take it as soon as they remember, and continue on the schedule. Those who forget two or three also are often encouraged to take the omitted tablets and keep on going, but to use another form of contraception as a means of "extra insurance."

When The Pill was introduced, it was regarded as the ideal contraceptive. Its effectiveness was unquestioned (less than one pregnancy per one hundred women over a year if taken according to schedule), and it was a method completely apart from sexual intercourse. A woman could swallow a tablet with her coffee in the morning or with her tomato juice at night. It was all part of her daily routine and had nothing to do with sex.

It's hardly a surprise that The Pill caught on as quickly as it did. Over a third of women using a form of birth control today are taking some form of oral contraceptive—and fully half of the wives under age thirty choose this method. Even a larger percentage have *tried* it but did not like it. Many women complain of the short-term side effects: a bloated feeling, nausea, vomiting, spotting between menstrual periods, breast discomfort, weight gain or loss, changes in sex interest, headaches, nervousness, fatigue, and a variety of other relatively minor effects. Many of these symptoms are much like those of early pregnancy and often disappear after completion of a few pill cycles. But there are some serious problems that have been associated with the oral contraceptive, and you should know about them, too.

Studies in the United States and Great Britain have shown that there is a relationship between oral contraceptive use and blood clotting. Women using The Pill assume up to eleven times the risk of non-Pill takers of developing clotting problems. Some three of every 100,000 women taking The Pill die each year from Pill-related causes, and it is estimated that one woman in every 2,000 on The Pill each year suffers a blood-clotting disorder serious enough to require hospitalization.

Because of the possiblility of these medical problems, oral contraceptives are available only through a physician's pre-scription, and only after the woman has been given a physical examination to learn if there is some reason why she should not be taking The Pill.

Any woman using The Pill who has severe leg or chest pains, coughs up blood, has difficulty breathing, experiences sudden se-vere headache or vomiting, dizziness, or fainting, disturbances of vision or speech, weakness or numbness of an arm or leg should call her doctor and immediately stop taking The Pill. These symptoms occur very infrequently, but both a husband and wife will want to be aware of any possible problem signs.

Some couples, after hearing about the possible things that can happen to women who are on The Pill, decide that the advantages offered by this means of birth control are just not worth the risk, minimal though it is. But others feel fully confident about using the oral contraceptive. It's really a matter of choice. A woman choosing this method should recognize that The Pill can have more serious side effects than most means of birth control, and she should satisfy herself that she is achieving sufficient unique benefit from its use to justify those risks.

Birth-Control Shots

You may have heard about the birth-control shots that are designed to provide contraception protection for an extended time period—perhaps a month, even three months. The contraceptive shot introduces into the woman's body time-released hormones that gradually send chemicals into her bloodstream. These hormones inhibit ovulation (or in some other way prevent pregnancy) without necessitating daily pill-taking discipline. They've been proven to be about as effective as The Pill.

But nothing is perfect. The primary problem with the injectable contraceptives is the complete disorganization of the menstrual cycle that accompanies their use. Depending on the type of drug being used, menstrual bleeding can be completely absent or may occur on just about every day of the menstrual cycle. No month is quite the same. This type of irregularity poses problems for some women. The failure to menstruate is often associated with pregnancy and some women panic when bleeding does not occur. Some misled women are concerned because they interpret the lack of a menstrual period as a sign that "toxic material" is being kept inside them. On the other hand, excessive menstruation, quite simply, can be a nuisance.

In addition there is some evidence that there can be a significant delay in the return of fertility after using the injectables. For this reason and other reasons, birth-control shots are not widely used in this country. When they are, they are most often offered to women who have completed their families.

Female Sterilization

The Pill, birth-control shots, and the forms of female sterilization prevent the egg from making its journey toward the uterus. The Pill and shots usually prevent the egg from being released from the ovary in the first place. Female sterilization does not interfere with the egg being released, but it creates a situation in which the egg cannot complete its passage down the fallopian tube toward the uterus.

There are two popular forms of female sterilization. *Tubal ligation*, or "having the tubes tied," the more familiar of the two means, is the cutting and tying of the two fallopian tubes so that the egg cannot complete its journey from the ovary to the uterus. Tubal ligation is a highly effective means of birth control (as effective as the Pill) but has the disadvantage of being a fairly complicated surgical procedure involving abdominal incisions to gain access to the tubes.

A newer technique is *laparoscopic sterilization*. A laparoscope is a thin, stainless-steel tube, which can be inserted through the abdominal wall, just below the navel. An intense light at the end of the tube allows the physician to see the internal reproductive organs and identify each of the two oviducts. A small piece of tissue is "snipped" from each oviduct and the ends of each are sealed. Where the specialized equipment is available, this operation can often be done within about fifteen minutes, using just local anesthetic. Some women can go about their business as usual; others experience menstrual-like cramps and need a few days of home rest for total recovery. Laparoscopic sterilization (and a similar method called *culdoscopy*, in which the tubes are reached through the vagina, without abdominal incisions) are currently being perfected and soon may be the universally preferable means of female sterilization.

All types of sterilization are reserved for those couples who are very sure they want no more children. These methods seem particularly well suited for women in their middle or late thirties who have completed their families (and maybe even had more children than they had anticipated). At thirty-five, for instance, a woman may well have ten fertile years left. She may not want to take even the small risk of pregnancy that's associated with mechanical means of birth control and in her case, her physician may feel that ten consecutive years of taking the oral contraceptive could present health hazards. Sterilization indeed may be the method for her, offering complete pregnancy protection without interfering with ovulation, menstruation, or sexual enjoyment.

In 1970, some 7 percent of all married women—and over 13

percent of married women between thirty and forty-four—had chosen some form of female sterilization.

KEEPING THE SPERM OUT

Withdrawal

One of the oldest forms of birth control (one mentioned in both the Book of Genesis and the Talmud) is *coitus interruptus,* also known as *withdrawal.* This method requires a man to withdraw his penis from the woman's vagina before he has an ejaculation.

Withdrawal was probably the first soundly scientific means of avoiding conceptions. Its use acknowledged that male semen was necessary for pregnancy to occur and that the chances of a conception would be reduced if semen could be kept out of the woman's body. There were no fancy devices or chemical preparations necessary for the use of this method, and no serious side effects. So, in the absence of any better method, withdrawal became very popular.

But couples depending on this approach to conception control also found out that it was not the easiest method to use—and it certainly could *not* be described as a "foolproof" means of birth control.

What made it difficult to use was that the moment of male orgasm is not always easy to predict. And even when it could be predicted, the motivation to withdraw at the height of sexual excitement was often lacking. What made it less foolproof was that sperm can escape from the man's urethra prior to the actual orgasm—and thus conception might take place despite withdrawal. The problems associated with withdrawal as a means of birth control explain why less than 2 percent of married couples in this country use this means of family planning.

It is difficult to give statistics on the effectiveness of withdrawal among couples who do choose to rely on it. First, the types of couples choosing this method probably are less motivated to avoid pregnancy than are those choosing more sophisticated techniques. They, therefore, may have failures with *any* means of birth control. Second, it appears that the failure of the withdrawal method to prevent an unwanted pregnancy more likely stems from the fact that the method was misused (that is, the man did not withdraw before he had orgasm), rather than to a problem related to the method itself (only rarely would enough sperm be released in sufficient quantities in the pre-ejaculation secretions to cause pregnancy).

One study showed that eighteen of every one hundred women whose husbands practiced coitus interruptus for a full year became pregnant. Based on this and other observations, most physicians now feel that whatever the cause of the "accident," the withdrawal method, while better than no method at all, is not a very effective form of birth control.

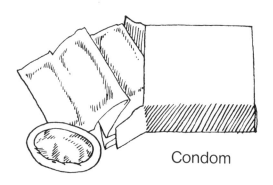

Condom

Condom

The condom is another method that is designed to prevent pregnancy by keeping the sperm from entering the vagina.

Reference to the condom (alternately referred to as a rubber, a sheath, an English riding coat, an assurance cap, or a French letter) are found throughout medical history books. Greeks wore condomlike sheaths as a form of decoration. Primitive tribes used a type of penis covering as protection against insect bites.

One theory about the origin of the condom as a contraceptive device revolves around a seventeenth-century physician named Dr. Condom who was said to have developed this method as a favor for one of his patients who was a member of royalty. But it is more likely that the name comes from the Latin word *condus*, meaning "receptacle," because that is really what a condom is—a receptacle for semen once it is released from the man's penis.

Today we think of the condom as a male form of birth control. But actually, early condomlike methods were designed for women. Wives not wanting to conceive would line their vaginas with a baglike device (possibly made from linen or animal tissues) so that the sperm could be caught as it was released. In 1564, however, an Italian medical researcher recommended the use of a linen sheath to be placed on the penis (originally as a means of protection against syphilis). But this invention had the distinct disadvantage of reducing the pleasurable type of sensation that usually accompanied sexual intercourse. (One early critic of the condom wrote, "I do not care to shut myself up in a piece of dead skin to prove that I am perfectly alive.")

Condoms didn't become popular and practical as a means of birth control until the vulcanization of rubber in the mid-nineteenth century (Charles Goodyear developed this process in 1839) made it possible to produce a condom that was both thin and strong. After that condoms became more effective, easily handled, and detracted less from the enjoyment of sex.

Today's condoms are made of thin, but very strong, synthetic rubber. ("Skin" condoms that are made of gut are still available, but are much more expensive than the latex ones.) The Food and Drug Administration now requires that condom production be strictly supervised to ensure that the products are free from any types of imperfection, particularly holes or points of weakness. The effectiveness of the condom is reflected in the statistics that somewhere between five and fifteen pregnancies occur per year among every one hundred couples using this method, and it is probable that a significant number of these failures resulted from the decision to omit the device "just once."

In addition to its effectiveness as a means of preventing conception, the condom offers two other advantages over some other means of birth control, which we will discuss later. First, condoms are available at most drugstores and can be purchased without a doctor's prescription. Second, condoms are not associated with any adverse medical side effects, because their action is local and other areas of the body are not affected.

But the condom is not the ideal means of birth control for all couples. Some don't like the idea of interrupting the sex act to put it in place (the condom can't be properly positioned until after the man has a full erection). Others complain that no matter how thin and uncumbersome the device is, its presence is still felt and they are aware that "something" is preventing full, intimate contact. These objections have moved the condom to the number two position in the contraceptive popularity ratings, with about 11 percent of young married couples choosing this method.

Vasectomy (Male Sterilization)

The third family-planning approach designed to keep the sperm from entering the female vagina is *vasectomy*, or male sterilization. But before you can understand what a vasectomy is and how it is effective in preventing conception, you must recall some facts about male reproductive physiology discussed in Chapter 2.

You remember that sperm are manufactured in the tubes of the testes and then enter the epididymis to mature. They begin their "outbound" journey by moving from the epididymis, along the vas deferens, and into the sperm reservoir. Before they are released, they enter the ejaculatory duct and join with the secretions of the prostate gland and seminal vesicles. Finally, they are released from the body through the urethra in the form of semen.

The first important fact to remember is that the sperm represent just one part of the semen. The greatest portion of the semen is accounted for by the secretions from the internal male organs —not by the sperm. The second important fact to focus on is that a man must have a complete anatomical highway before the sperm can make the full journey from the testes to the outside world. If that highway is interrupted in some way, the sperm cannot move along.

This is the idea behind vasectomy. The operation, unlike the most popular forms of female sterilization, is usually performed in a physician's office on an out-patient basis—that is, no hospitalization is necessary. The doctor first injects a local painkiller and makes two small incisions in each of the scrotal sacs so that he can gain access to the vas ducts. The cutting, tying, and mending of the incision take just a few minutes, and the procedure is then complete. The man may be advised to use another form of contraception for a few weeks to give the sperm already in the upper portion of the vas deferens and reservoir a chance to escape. Thereafter, however, he need not worry about producing children again.

Some misinformed men think that they would lose their "manliness" if they had a vasectomy. Actually, they may be confusing vasectomy with castration, a very rarely performed operation in which the testes are removed. After a vasectomy, a man's reproductive processes continue as usual. He has a regular orgasm with the release of semen, but the semen soon becomes sperm-free. The sperm that are manufactured in the testes cannot make the upward climb and quickly disintegrate.

Vasectomy is a relatively simple operation, but is one that a man will want to think about carefully before he decides to have it since generally the procedure is not reversible. There are cases where physicians have been able to reunite the two portions of the vas, but this is not something a man can count on. Sterilization— whether it is the male or female variety—should be considered as a permanent form of birth control, and should be reserved for couples who are confident that they want to have no more children of their own.

Vasectomy has become increasingly popular in the United States over the past few years. In 1970 over 8 percent of all couples using some form of family planning—and 12 percent of those in which the wife was between the ages of thirty and forty-four—reported vasectomy was their current method of conception control. The popularity of vasectomy is particularly great among couples living on the West Coast. A recent study of a suburban California population showed that almost one-fifth (18 percent) of couples in which the wife was between the ages of forty and fifty-four had chosen vasectomy.

KEEPING THE SPERM OUT—SOMETIMES

The Rhythm Method

Withdrawal, the condom, and vasectomy are all attempts to keep sperm from entering the vagina. The rhythm method has the same general goal, but is concerned only with keeping the woman's body sperm-free during the days of the menstrual cycle when conception is most likely to occur. The manner in which sperm are kept out is sexual abstinence—that is, the couple refrains from intercourse for a number of days.

Scientists have talked about a "rhythm method" for many centuries, but even well into this century, as pointed out in an earlier chapter, the fertile or pregnancy period was thought to be during the menstrual flow! Some animals bleed when they are "in heat" and likely to conceive, so it was assumed that women did also.

In 1930, doctors in Japan and Austria independently discovered the facts that are now behind our current understanding of the practice of the rhythm method and showed us that the popular belief was wrong!

Before we go into the details of the practice of the rhythm method, you should be aware that a significant portion (but not all) of the couples choosing this method do so for religious reasons. It is the only birth-control method condoned by the Roman Catholic Church. But often couples are interested in the rules of the rhythm method for reasons unrelated to religion. A solid understanding of the principles behind the two types of rhythm regulation can make mechanical contraception more effective. To be very safe, for instance, a couple using a condom might keep track of the fertile period and avoid intercourse on the days that appear particularly pregnancy-prone. Rhythm for them is just an extra measure of insurance.

The rhythm method is based on the basic principles of reproductive physiology that you have already read about. A woman is at risk of pregnancy for only about three or four days per month. Successful use of rhythm involves the identification of those days and the avoidance of sexual intercourse during them. If it were just those three or four days that were involved, rhythm probably would be much more popular than it is. But it doesn't work that way. Unpredictable irregularities in the length of a woman's menstrual cycle require abstinence for several days on either side of the "likely fertile period."

If a woman has a regular thirty-day cycle, she might make the following calculations:

sperm- survival days ♂		MARCH					
		1●	**2●**	**3●**	**4●**	**5●**	
6	7	8	9	1 0	1 1	1 2	likely time ♀
1 3	(14)↗	(15)↗	(16)↗ +	(17)+	1 8	1 9	of ovulation
2 0	2 1	2 2	2 3	2 4	2 5	2 6	
2 7	2 8	2 9	3 0	**31●**			menstrual bleeding●

sperm- survival days ♂		APRIL					
					1●	**2●**	likely time ♀ of ovulation
3●	**4●**	5	6	7	8	9	
1 0	1 1	1 2	(13)↗	(14)↗	(15) +	(16) +	
1 7	1 8	1 9	2 0	2 1	2 2	2 3	
2 4	2 5	2 6	2 7	2 8	2 9	**30●**	menstrual bleeding●

The March "possible pregnancy period" would cover March 14, 15, 16, and 17. The April unsafe time would be April 13, 14, 15, and 16.

But this is a hypothetical woman. She's not subject to emotional or physical stress that could throw her day of ovulation off by a day, three days, a week, or even longer. To avoid pregnancy successfully, the real-life woman using rhythm has to avoid intercourse for a considerable portion of the month. The popular formula for detecting the really safe period is as follows:

1. Keep track of cycle lengths for about a year.
2. Subtract *18* from the shortest cycle length and *11* from the longest cycle length.
3. *THESE DAYS AND THE DAYS IN BETWEEN MAKE UP THE "UNSAFE" PERIOD.*

For instance, take the case of the make-believe lady above. Maybe the "regular" thirty-day cycle is actually just her average cycle length. Perhaps her cycles vary in length from twenty-six days to thirty-two days. Her calculations would be as follows:

Shortest Cycle		Longest Cycle
26		32
− 18		− 11
day 8	to	day 21

Days eight and twenty-one, and the days in between them, represent her unsafe period. In order for her to practice strict calendar rhythm, she would have to avoid intercourse for fourteen consecutive days. Needless to say, calendar rhythm is not the most popular of birth-control methods among married couples—especially where the wife has irregular menstrual cycles.

A definitely more scientific approach to rhythm method involves the use of a *basal-body-temperature thermometer*, a special type of thermometer that shows even the smallest shifts in body temperature.

During the course of the menstrual cycle, a woman experiences shifts in her temperature. These shifts are related to changes in levels of her hormones.

If she plots out her temperature throughout the whole menstrual cycle (not at any time of the day, but specifically at the very moment she wakes up in the morning), she will notice that it is relatively low during the first half of the cycle, then it dips some, and all of a sudden goes up about a degree or more. The upward shift in temperature is believed to indicate that ovulation is occurring or has occurred. As you remember, at the time of ovulation the hormone progesterone begins to be produced in significant quantities. Progesterone has a "thermodynamic" effect—that is, it causes the temperature to rise.

The rise in body temperature, as long as it stays up for a few days, will confirm that ovulation has occurred. Strict use of basal-body-temperature rhythm does not allow intercourse from the time of the end of the menstrual flow to three full days after the rise in temperature—that is, until the beginning of the fourth day.

According to this schedule, the woman with a thirty-day cycle would avoid intercourse for about twelve consecutive days. But even then, her efforts could be thwarted by some kind of infection (even a cold) that could make her temperature go up for a reason not related to ovulation.

Statistics indicate that calendar rhythm is one of the least effective of birth-control efforts (with some twenty-four pregnancies per hundred women over a given year). Probably the main reason this method has such a high failure rate is that people don't follow the rules closely enough. The effectiveness of temperature rhythm is very much greater. If this method is carefully used, the pregnancy rate is less than two per one hundred women per year.

But both forms of rhythm do require a great deal of bookkeeping and a significant amount of self-restraint. And because of all its disadvantages, only 4 percent of young married couples use this method.

"ROADBLOCK" CONTRACEPTIVES

When our scientifically oriented ancestors concluded that it was the presence of sperm in a woman's body that initiated a pregnancy, they set out to devise methods that either would kill sperm or prevent them from going beyond the woman's vagina. Basically, they developed a "roadblock," which a woman could insert in her vagina to frustrate the traveling efforts of the sperm. The problem was that some of these mechanical or chemical roadblocks were not all that attractive.

Aristotle recommended the use of oil of cedar, sometimes mixed with olive oil. Egyptians recommended the use of a vaginal plug made with crocodile dung, grasses, seaweeds, dried figs, or beeswax. Many of these methods were not effective at all, and the physicians prescribing them usually visited their patients about nine months later to deliver their babies. But some of them *were* very effective and were really the forerunners of two of our "modern" methods, the diaphragm and sperm killers.

Early primitive women who used leaves soaked with a substance such as lemon juice, alcohol, or vinegar may indeed have experienced the desired effect if these preparations were sufficiently acidic to incapacitate the sperm. Women using oil or honey may have had some luck also by creating a sticky environment, one that the sperm did not have the power to penetrate.

Diaphragm

In 1882, a German physician devised a more aesthetically pleasing version of the crocodile dung-roadblock method when he created a shallow rubber cup, which was designed to cover the neck of the uterus and prevent sperm from entering.

The modern diaphragm is a latex-rubber, dome-shaped cup, which can range from two to four inches in diameter. The differences in size allow the physician to select a device that is appropriate for the size and contour of a woman's vagina. A spring in the outside rim makes the device easy to manipulate during insertion or removal, and keeps it securely in place, fully covering the entrance to the uterus.

The diaphragm serves its contraceptive function in two distinct ways. First, it acts as a roadblock so sperm cannot get through the cervix. Second, it provides a storage space for spermicidal (sperm-killing) preparations, which makes life very difficult for sperm when they enter the vagina. These spermicides are essential if the diaphragm is to be effective in preventing conception.

When it is correctly used, the diaphragm is inserted into the vagina so that the bowl portion, which holds the sperm-killing preparations, is facing the uterus. It can be placed in this position up to six hours before intercourse. But if it has been more than six hours since insertion, or if sexual intercourse is repeated, it is necessary to put in a new spermicide. This is done with a special type of plunger-inserter, so that the diaphragm itself does not have to be removed. Particularly if intercourse has just recently taken place, the device should definitely not be removed. The diaphragm must be left in place for six to eight hours after intercourse takes place, just to make sure no sperm are still alive.

The diaphragm-with-spermicide method is highly effective (as few as two women per one hundred per year become pregnant if they use it properly), and it has no significant medical side effects. But it is not "the answer" for all women. Indeed, only about 4 percent of young married couples in the United States now use it.

Some couples feel that the diaphragm, when compared to The

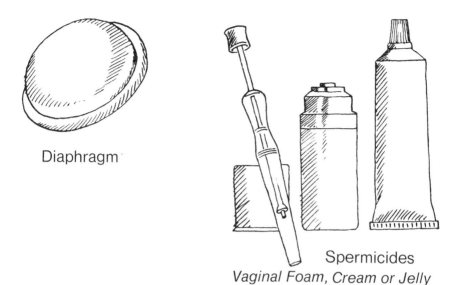

Diaphragm

Spermicides
Vaginal Foam, Cream or Jelly

Pill, is messy and difficult to use. Others, when they compare it to the condom, say it has the disadvantage of requiring a doctor's prescription and the associated expense. Others don't like to be so premeditated about sex, and resent having to interrupt any spontaneity to insert the device. And some women just do not like to touch their sex organs or are never able to convince themselves that the device is in the way it should be.

Contraceptive Spermicides

Another way of both blocking the sperm's entrance to the vagina and killing these little cells at the same time is the "spermicides alone" method. Spermicides come in the form of creams, gels, or foam. All of these substances are put in a special plastic applicator (some come prefilled which can be easily inserted into the vagina, much like a tampon. These substances can be inserted up to an hour before intercourse, but if intercourse occurs after this hour interval, or if sex is repeated, a whole new application of the spermicide is necessary.

Spermicidal preparations offer the distinct advantage of being readily available at the local drugstore without a doctor's prescription. They are considered less effective when used alone than when used with a diaphragm (a failure rate of around ten to twenty pregnancies per one hundred women in a year). But if used properly, spermicides, particularly those in the form of foam, can offer a significant amount of protection from conception without any major side effects. About 8 percent of young married American couples using contraceptives see enough advantages in spermicidal preparations to choose them as their means of conception control. Many others, however, find the creams, foams, and gels messy and unpleasant to use, and prefer not to depend on a method that requires so much attention before sexual intercourse.

The Mini-Pill

You might be surprised to see mention of a pill in the section discusing birth-control methods that block the sperm from entering the cervix. But it seems that this is how the mini-pill offers contraceptive protection—or at least one of the ways it does.

The mini-pill received its name not because it is unusually small, but because, unlike the original birth-control pill, it contains only one hormone. The one hormone is a synthetic form of progesterone. The mini-pill contains no estrogen, which recently has been identified as the villain in pill-related blood clotting.

As we pointed out earlier, during the course of a woman's menstrual cycle, the secretions around the cervix change in consistency. Around ovulation, for instance, the secretions are thin and watery, and sperm find it relatively easy to pass through on their way into the uterus and oviducts. After ovulation, the cervical secretions are thick, sticky, and profuse, and themselves act as a sperm roadblock. The mini-pill attempts to simulate the natural sperm-blocking nature of the postovulatory cervical secretions. When a woman takes her daily mini-pill, her cervix builds up a natural sperm defense system.

The mini-pill is very effective if it is taken regularly. But while a woman might "get away" with forgetting the traditional type of birth-control pill, she might become pregnant after just one pill is missed—because of the mini-action of this drug. This is a problem for some women. Additionally, the mini-pill does bring about some changes in menstrual bleeding, and some women cannot tolerate this.

The Mystery Method: The Intrauterine Device

Coitus interruptus and vasectomy prevent conception by keeping the sperm from entering the vagina. Calendar and temperature rhythm focus on keeping the woman's body sperm free during her fertile period. The diaphragm, spermicides, and the mini-pill block the sperm's efforts to pass through the cervix into the uterus. The oral contraceptives and birth-control shots prevent an egg from making its monthly appearance or in some other way affect conception or implantation. Female sterilization interferes with the normal journey of the egg from the ovary to the uterus. They all prevent the egg and the sperm from getting together. But no one is quite sure how the *intrauterine devices*—or IUDs—work to prevent pregnancies. All we know is that they do work—most of the time. And about 9 percent of young married couples choose this method.

For many centuries it has been known that conception in animals could be prevented by placing some foreign material in the uterus. Arab tribes used to place a stone in the uterus of camels before beginning their long desert crossings. As a result, no baby camels were born. In the early part of this century a German physician decided to find out if a uterine device could prevent pregnancies in women also. He invented a small ringlike coil, which did have the desired effect, but was not well accepted because of the widespread, uncontrollable infections that often occurred (and there were no antibiotics then to handle this problem). But with today's IUDs, infection is less of a problem, and in the rare cases it does occur, drugs are available to control it.

Today's IUDs, whether they are in the form of a loop, ring, or spiral, are usually made of a flexible polyethylene plastic, which has the capacity to "remember" its shape after being stretched out into a straight line. The physician (or a specially trained nurse) places the device in a strawlike tube inserter and introduces it through the vagina and cervix into the uterus. When in the uterus, the plunger on the inserter is pushed and the intrauterine device slowly emerges, assuming its original shape as it comes out. A small string is left to hang through the cervix both to facilitate its removal and to allow the woman to check occasionally to ensure that the device is still where it should be.

How the IUD works is still uncertain. It's a mysterious method,

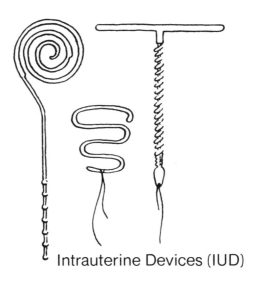

Intrauterine Devices (IUD)

which seems to prevent babies in the same manner in which it prevented baby camels. Early researchers thought that the device changed the nature of the inside lining of the uterus so that implantation could not occur. Others, however, have suggested that the presence of the IUD has the effect of accelerating the movement of the egg down the oviduct so much that the uterine lining has not been prepared sufficiently to receive it.

More recently, scientists have suggested that the IUD causes a "foreign body" reaction in the uterus, stimulating increased secretions of uterine fluid so that the circumstances for implantation are less than ideal. And there is still another explanation: Maybe more than one of these mechanisms work together to prevent pregnancy, especially when copper or some other element is added to the IUD.

As was the case with The Pill, the IUD was originally considered to be the ideal contraceptive. It was inexpensive and required little attention by the woman. But the IUD does involve problems. Some women have it removed because of heavy bleeding and pain. Others just don't like the idea of "having something inside them." And a small percentage of others—perhaps three of every one hundred women who use it for a year—do become pregnant. (When pregnancy does occur, the presence of the device appears not to bother the growing baby.) In some cases, IUDs have been associated with perforation of the uterus (that is, the piercing of the inside of that organ) and with infections. And one particular IUD was recently reviewed by the FDA because it could present more serious risks—and had been associated with the death of a very small number of women.

OLD AND NEW, AND NOT RECOMMENDED

Douche

Even as a primitive woman thought she could "shake out all the sperm" by jumping up and down after sexual intercourse, so do some modern women think that they can flush out sperm by *douching*, that is, washing out their vagina with a solution introduced with a syringelike device. But unfortunately for them, this method does not work.

Sperm are independent cells, and they start their journey right after they are released into the woman's body. Actually, some scientists feel that douching and the associated water pressure may even give the sperm an extra push in the direction they want to go.

Morning-After Pill

Perhaps you have heard of the so-called "morning-after pill," medication to be taken after intercourse to interrupt a pregnancy if one has occurred. The morning-after pill is basically a large dose of estrogen, which may be administered within about forty-eight hours after a woman has had unprotected intercourse during her fertile period. It appears that the morning-after pill affects the lining of the uterus and therefore interferes with the fertilized egg's efforts to settle there.

But morning-after pills are not used routinely. Physicians will use them only as a real emergency method—for instance, in the case of rape. Even then they probably will want to make sure that intercourse took place during a fertile (or possibly fertile) portion of the menstrual cycle before they administer the drug. The great hesitation about the use of the morning-after pill is related to problems associated with its major ingredient, DES (the abbreviation for diethylstilbestrol), which has been linked with a very rare form of vaginal cancer. While it's not likely that one morning-after treatment would lead to this problem, the mere possibility of such a risk warrants limited use of the morning-after drug.

Abortion

Throughout history, abortion—that is, the induced termination of a pregnancy already in process—as well as infanticide has headed the list of birth-control methods. The early attempts at pregnancy interruption were very crude, and put the mother's life in danger. Modern techniques of abortion are much safer, but abortion still remains on the "not recommended list," because of physical, psychological, and moral problems.

Until recently, abortions were performed almost exclusively by means of the *dilation and curettage* (or D&C) method. A curette is a small, spoon-shaped instrument, which can be inserted through a dilated (open) cervix to scrape away the embryonic tissues. D&Cs are usually not performed beyond the third month of pregnancy because of the serious dangers associated with perforation of the tissues of the uterus. When a pregnancy has proceeded beyond this time (particularly if more than sixteen weeks has elapsed), the *saline induction* method may be used: A small amount of a salt solution is injected through the abdominal wall to kill the fetus. Under ideal conditions, the dead fetus will be expelled almost immediately, but often the expulsion is delayed for many hours. The psychological ramifications of carrying around a dead fetus makes this method particularly unacceptable to many women.

The increase in the number of legal abortions in the United States has resulted in wider use of the *abortion aspirator*, a suction-pump device that can be introduced into the uterus through the vagina. As was the case with the D&C technique, the uterine tissues are scraped away, but the aspirator accumulates the materials as the operation proceeds.

A significant number of American couples now believe that it is a woman's right to terminate a pregnancy if it is not wanted. The Supreme Court of the United States agreed with them in January, 1973, when it decided that existing state anti-abortion laws were generally unconstitutional. The decision specifically stated that up to the end of the first trimester of pregnancy (usually defined as the first thirteen weeks of gestation), the decision to have an abortion may be made solely by the pregnant woman and her doctor. Following the end of the first trimester, the state can regulate the abortion procedure—but only to the extent that is reasonable for protecting maternal and child health. Only after the "point of viability"—defined by the court as being somewhere between the twenty-fourth to twenty-eighth week of pregnancy—does a state have the real authority to control abortion.

But abortion—legal or not—is still a very controversial subject. People on either side of the question, however, do agree that it is not a recommended form of birth control. There is concern that abortion will be overused as an alternative to preventive family planning. Abortion has been legal in a significant number of countries for many years: Russia, Japan, China, Poland, Czechoslovakia, Hungary, Bulgaria, and Yugoslavia, for instance, have reported a tremendous number of abortions. In Hungary the number of abortions officially reported is considerably higher than the number of births. During the first year following the liberalization of abortion in New York City, there was nearly one city resident abortion performed for every two resident live births.

The great extent of utilization of abortion—in spite of the availability of a wide choice of effective contraceptives—is a source of concern for at least two reasons. First, there is statistical evidence that abortions accomplished by means of the popular D&C method can lead to problems in subsequent pregnancies. A British study recently revealed that women having their pregnancies terminated by D&Cs were ten times more likely than nonaborted women—or women who had lost their babies naturally—to have a spontaneous miscarriage during the second trimester (between about the third and sixth month) of their subsequent pregnancies. It seems that there can be some temporary or permanent damage done during the course of the abortion, and the cervix becomes unable to perform its important function, namely to prevent the fetus from being expelled prematurely.

Second, there is the feeling that repeated use of pregnancy termination as a means of birth control is both morally unhealthy and aesthetically displeasing, and has the possibility of creating a disturbing complacency about the value of human life.

BIRTH CONTROL AND THE FUTURE

There is not yet an "ideal" form of contraception. And so the research goes on. Some investigators are concentrating their efforts on improving methods that already exist. Others are looking in new directions and, as a change of emphasis, are giving particular attention to the *male* role in contraception.

New IUDs and Safer Pills

The next "generation" of IUDs will have some new characteristics, ones that might make this form of contraception more effective and attractive. Particularly, an IUD that is embedded with copper has been devised and is now being tested. The copper is continuously eroded from the IUD into the uterus, where it serves as an antifertility agent. This type of copper-releasing IUD appears to be more effective than the regular type—and seems to be associated with a lower incidence of patient discomfort.

And research is going on to improve the existing forms of oral contraceptives (although many people still maintain that scientists can never beat the efficiency of nature's oral contraceptive—the word "no!"). One approach involves the reduction in the amounts of hormones that go into The Pill, the idea being that the side effects will be reduced if the medication dosage is less. Additionally, a "once-a-month pill" has been developed and has been successfully used in Latin America and in other countries. This pill acts much like an injection in that it slowly releases hormones into a woman's bloodstream.

In addition to the use of pills, attention is being given to the possibility of using hormones that are introduced into the woman's body in another fashion. One such device is the *intravaginal ring*, which is placed in the vagina in the same position as a diaphragm would be. The ring then releases hormones into the body at a level high enough to prevent pregnancy. Similarly, attention is being given to the possibility that hormones can be released through *subdermal implants,* which are placed under the skin.

Male Methods

You've probably noticed that our discussion of modern birth-control methods has focused almost exclusively on the female. A researcher in the contraceptive field once referred to birth-control research as "a male chauvinist plot." But there *is* interest in the male. The problem seems to be that the number of "targets" in the male reproductive system are limited.

It is known that the same hormones that can block ovulation in women can block spermatogenesis in men. But there are some very unacceptable side effects, namely that the man's testosterone levels drop to near zero, and his sex drive almost completely disappears. Similarly, it is known that testosterone and other male hormones (androgens) can stop sperm production in men, but, on the other hand, it is also known that high androgen levels in the blood can increase the probability of heart attacks. (As a matter of fact, many doctors believe that the presence of these male hormones explains why men have somewhat shorter life spans than women.)

And there can be some other problems, too. In 1960, a team of scientists thought they had the perfect male pill. They tried it out on some volunteers in a prison, and found that sperm production was reduced to amazingly low levels. So they tried it out on a general population, only to uncover some unexpected results. The nonprison volunteers often got sick—they were dizzy, had nausea, and often vomited. The puzzle was solved when it was pointed out that the second set of male volunteers, unlike the prison population, were drinking alcoholic beverages, and the combination of the drug and the drinks made them ill. But even more important than this, in the later evaluation of this male pill it was found that the few sperm that were available in semen were abnormal. And abnormal sperm, like abnormal eggs, can contribute to the possibility of a genetically imperfect baby.

In addition to investigating the possibility of antifertility medication for males, attention is being given to the possibility of developing techniques for a reversible vasectomy. Perhaps soon a man undergoing a "vasectomy," instead of having his vas deferens cut and tied, will have it blocked with the use of a plug, valve, or clip that can eventually be removed.

CONTRACEPTION AND MOTIVATION

Whatever the birth control of tomorrow will be, its success will still depend on two very important elements—motivation and commitment on behalf of *both* the husband and wife using it. Too often people assume that when a "super method" is developed, couples will automatically use it properly and regularly. But even the most sophisticated and acceptable birth-control drug or device is not going to work without a heavy dose of motivation from the couples using it. And that applies to both members of the couple! We have moved beyond the point where we would consider birth control as being the responsibility of just the husband or just the wife. It is a joint responsibility.

BEYOND TESTES AND OVARIES

You are probably aware now, having read about all the details of reproductive physiology and its control, that we are living in an age in which we know more than ever about our bodies and how to prevent the occurrence of unwanted pregnancy. When you are married, and the time comes for you to decide about parenthood, you first will be able to decide whether you want babies at all, and then you can choose when and how often babies come into your life. You even may have the option to choose the sex of your offspring.

You have the "facts of life," that is, the *biological* facts of life. But there is more—much more—to sex and human reproduction than elements of anatomy and physiology. Having sexual intercourse and becoming a parent involve a very serious decision-making process. These are both very special events, ones that most men and women want to reserve for the right time, place, and person. So that you can really have a complete sex education, let's now turn our attention to some nonbiological sex issues, specifically those that will help you determine the "when" and "why" of sexual activity and parenthood.

chapter 7

A New Look at "Sexual Freedom"

"OF COURSE I KNOW EVERY-
THING ABOUT SEX!"

A well-known New York psychiatrist reports that he once asked a sixteen-year-old-boy, "Do you know the meaning of sex?" The boy looked at him in astonishment, probably wondering how any doctor could think a boy could live for sixteen years and *not* have all the answers about sex. He responded indignantly, "Of course I do! I know all about erections and seminal emissions. And I know about what happens during a woman's menstrual cycle, and about how babies are made and prevented. What else is there to know?"

Actually, there is a great deal more to know about sex, because this is one subject that definitely goes beyond the biology books. For humans, sexual intercourse is more than the primary way a new life is created. It is more than a means of satisfying a physical need. It is the way in which two people who love and respect each other can share a wide range of both physical and emotional feelings in the closest relationship two human beings are capable of achieving. Sexual intercourse is the supreme example of an interpersonal relationship.

Let's pause for a moment to compare some of the aspects of human sexuality to that of lower animals. In most animals, intercourse takes place only during one phase of the female's reproductive cycle—that is, when she is in "heat." You may have seen what happens when a female dog, for instance, is in heat. Male dogs from all over the neighborhood are attracted to her—and she is very interested in them. It is only during this phase of her cycle (technically known as the *estrous cycle*) that she will have sexual intercourse. Second, she is not very discriminating about which dog—it is more a matter of which one is available when she is interested.

There are at least three ways human sexuality is different. First, women can and do have sexual intercourse during all parts of their cycle. Some women are more interested in sex at one time than at another (scientific research has shown that many women are particularly responsive to sex in the days just before their menstrual period begins), but the fact remains, that in the human female, sexual activity is not restricted to one portion of the cycle.

Second, unlike the female cocker spaniel who is attracted to whatever male dog is in her neighborhood when she is in heat, humans are selective about their sex partners. This selectivity results from the fact that human sex is a psychological and emotional as well as a physical experience—and from the fact of life that intercourse does carry with it the possibility of pregnancy.

And third, humans enjoy a higher form of life than animals. We are interested in more than eating, sleeping, mating, and offspring. Sex and reproduction, although they are important, represent just one of our many priorities. We are interested in studying, learning, improving the quality of life for ourselves, for our friends, and for our descendants. One way we do that is by working and continuously accumulating information so we can pass it on to later generations.

SEX ATTITUDES AND RULES

We've described sex as "the supreme example of an interpersonal relationship." It's a very intimate and private relationship. But it is also inherently social. Think about it for a moment. There are two people involved. And there always remains the possibility that a third person might result from the relationship. So because sex is not an individual matter, societies, since earliest times, have had rules about when, where, and with whom intercourse should or could take place.

Of course these rules have not always been the same. Some societies, for instance, have been very restrictive about sexual activity—even when it was taking place in marriage. In American Puritan communities, for instance, married couples were forbidden to have intercourse on Sundays (if they did, they were to punish themselves by fasting for three full days). Similarly, throughout the eighteenth and nineteenth centuries, some physicians warned married couples against "sexual excess" and prescribed hard mattresses as the solution to "the problem."

With these types of sexual regulations and medical advice, it is not difficult to see why young men and women grew up thinking sex was evil, and that sex topics were not a legitimate subject of discussion. People just did not feel comfortable with discussions of sexual matters and avoided them wherever they could. For example, for centuries, a woman seeking help from her doctor was advised to bring a doll with her so that she could "point out the part that hurt" and avoid the possibility of using "unladylike" terminology.

This was one extreme in the rules about sex category. And as we know today, these attitudes that categorized sex as a four-letter word were unrealistic, and indeed unhealthy. But what about the other extreme? Have there been societies that have been totally permissive about sexual intercourse? Have there been cultures or times in history when sex was tolerated with anyone, anywhere, at any time?

The answer to this last sweeping question is no. As is the case with most rules set forth by society, they are necessary to protect the rights of the majority of people and they serve to make everyone's life a little more orderly and predictable.

Consider, for instance, the chaos that would result if everyone driving cars decided to ignore the traffic lights. Life on streets and highways would become very confusing and would remain that way until the rules and regulations were enforced. And consider what would happen if everyone felt free about having intercourse with whomever he or she chose. Husbands and wives would not enjoy the permanence and security of marriage. Children would not have a stable relationship with their parents—indeed, they might not know who their parents were.

There is a wide middle ground—even today—between the "thou shalt not, even in marriage" philosophy and the "everything goes" attitude. But where does our culture stand in this spectrum of ideas? What are our attitudes about sex?

A SHIFT IN ATTITUDE

If we were to answer these questions from the traditional point of view, we would have to say that the American society has always been very Victorian or puritanical about sex matters. As we mentioned in an earlier chapter, parents would tell their children "the stork brought you" or they would conjure up some equally fantastic story to deny the child the true facts about human reproduction. And if a teenager ever asked about the pros and cons of sexual intercourse before marriage, he or she would be given a two-letter response (NO!) with no clarifying explanation.

But things have changed, at least to some extent. We have exploded all those myths about the unnaturalness of sex. We no longer hesitate to give young adults the information they want and need about the physical changes of growing up and the events leading to conception, pregnancy, and birth and the techniques of birth control. The fact that you are reading this book is evidence of the new, open attitude toward this subject. We now openly acknowledge that sexual feelings and sexual behavior are very much a part of being human, and we know that a healthy, mature use of our sexuality is one of our most constructive human potentials.

So there certainly has been a shift of attitudes since the time when scientists were being criticized for studying the structure of the male sperm cells, and this shift did not happen gradually. It seems to have taken place in just a few years. For this reason, the whole transformation was given the name "the sexual revolution."

But what exactly is this so-called sexual revolution? And what impact is it having on our lives?

As we have discussed already, the sexual revolution has led us to be more honest about human sexuality and the positive role it plays in our lives. This point is clear. What is not so clear is its effect on our attitudes about the "when," "where," and "with whom" of sexual behavior. Does the sexual revolution mean that our traditional rules against premarital sex are irrelevant and unnecessary?

THE SEXUAL REVOLUTION: WHAT IS IT?

In the dictionary sense of the word, a revolution is a fundamental change, an overthrow or renunciation. With specific respect to the sexual revolution, it has been described as "a strong breeze of honesty that blew away many of the Victorian ideas about the unnaturalness of sex." The sexual revolution, however, does *not* mean that intercourse anywhere with anyone is now, for the first time in our history, perfectly acceptable. But if you look at the circumstances in which this change in attitude about sex occurred, you can see how some young people did become confused on this last point.

How did we make the transition from referring to sex in hushed tones to our current openness? And why did it all happen so quickly?

The first point to consider is that until very recently, young people derived their knowledge and attitudes only from their families and religious institutions. Of course, they did get some information from books, but the reproductive facts they received were very limited (one nineteenth-century book for teenage boys was entitled *Everything a Young Boy Must Know, But Not One Thing More)* and many of the stories they read reinforced the traditional view that premarital sex was wrong. (In the classic book, *The Scarlet Letter*, Nathaniel Hawthorne tells the story of Hester Prynne, who was doomed to wear the scarlet letter "A" for adultery so that people would know about her sexual transgressions.)

Throughout much of our history, young adults knew of just one life style—that is, the one in which sexual intercourse was reserved for marriage. Of course, there were always some teenagers who did not follow the rules and chose to engage in sexual activity, but they were in the minority.

In the 1950s, however, a communications innovation was introduced—television. Throughout the next twenty years, television shows became more and more candid in discussing many types of controversial issues, including premarital sexual behavior. Quite suddenly, young adults were learning about different life styles. On television, and in the movies, the life of the "swinging singles" looked very glamorous. Unfortunately, what some of these young adults did not realize was that what they saw on the screen could get them into trouble in the real world.

And it wasn't just television that had an effect on initiating the sexual revolution. Dating patterns among teenage men and women began to change. Although this may seem strange, dating as we know it today is a relatively new phenomenon. Before 1920, for instance, it just was not acceptable behavior to meet a girl and ask her for a date. A formal introduction was necessary, and when an unmarried couple did get together, they were well chaperoned. Only in the last few decades have young adults been given the freedom to be by themselves—in cars, at unchaperoned parties— and more sexual opportunities were available than before.

But there is still more background to the sexual revolution. Something else began to happen during the 1960s. People became concerned about world population growth. There was more discussion than ever before about birth control and the physiology of reproduction. The Pill was introduced and became widely used. And it suddenly appeared that sex could be truly separate from the possibility of pregnancy. While for generations young men had been warned not to have sexual intercourse before they were married because the girl might become pregnant, now they wondered, "If she is taking The Pill, what do I have to lose?"

SEXUAL FREEDOM IN THE AGE OF THE PILL

It was probably easier to handle the question of premarital sex when there were no super-sophisticated forms of contraception and when there were strict rules prohibiting teenage sex. The answer was just "no," and further discussion was unnecessary. A number of years ago, for instance, a young boy was asked, "What is keeping you from having sex with your girlfriend?" He responded, "The Establishment." When he was further asked, "What is the Establishment?" he responded, "My mother."

But it's very unlikely that you and your friends are going to settle for any answer from "the Establishment," whatever that term means to you. You want the facts, and you want to make your *own* decision about what role sex is going to play in your teenage life. You are living in an age in which we do have the freedom to choose, and you want to take advantage of that freedom. But before you make any important decision—especially one regarding sexual behavior—you should spend some time thinking about what the word "freedom" really means.

What do you think it means? Perhaps you are thinking freedom means, "I can do whatever I want to do." And some people today, although certainly not all, are applying this definition of freedom to sexuality. They have proclaimed themselves "sexually free," and have cast aside all forms of self-restraint.

But think about their behavior for a moment, and its possible consequences. What if these same people had the identical attitude about money? Say, for instance, a man was very wealthy, that he had one million dollars. Thinking that he was "free," he spent it without constraint. He didn't use the money constructively or discriminately, he just compulsively spent it whenever an opportunity presented itself. Is this man really free? No, of course he isn't. He is not thinking about his future. He is living for today and has become the slave of his unrestrained compulsion to spend.

People have different definitions of what freedom is, but you might be interested in those presented by two famous writers. Robert Frost wrote that "freedom is moving easy in a harness." Louis Ginsberg wrote that freedom was based on a series of restraints and, in his words, "Only in fetters is liberty; without its banks, what can a river be?"

So perhaps sexual freedom is not just "doing it" whenever you want to. It is making sound decisions about sex, being aware of the possible consequences that go with sexual behavior. And it is focusing on self-discipline and those "wise restraints that make men free."

ADVANTAGES AND CONSEQUENCES

We've already discussed sexual intercourse as being an intimate and emotional form of human behavior, one in which two people who love and respect each other can intimately share their feelings, both physically and emotionally. Sex is physically rewarding: The pleasurable sensations which accompany sexual stimulation, and eventually sexual release in orgasm, are both enjoyable and fulfilling. There is nothing wicked, shameful, and sinful about a mature, responsible sexual relationship. Sex is a positive, rewarding and enriching aspect of human life.

But the "mature" and "responsible" aspects of human sexuality must be there for the couple to derive this type of pleasure and reward—and for them to avoid the type of consequences that so often accompany the immature and irresponsible use of sexuality.

Not all teenagers today are given the whole story about sexual relationships. They know about the physical pleasure of sex and perhaps they know something about its emotional aspects, too. But those who have become convinced that sexual freedom means discarding the "old-fashioned hangups" about sex in favor of unrestrained sexual activity are not truly informed. Indeed, according to a growing number of psychologists and psychiatrists, these individuals are seeking a false freedom. They are electing to follow a life style of what appears to be sexual freedom, but they are being deprived of the knowledge of the consequences that often accompany sexual relationships that occur too early in life.

The late Dr. Max Levin, a former clinical professor of neurology at New York Medical College and practicing psychiatrist, described these uninformed individuals as "victims of a swindle." They are making one of the most important decisions in their lives without benefit of all the facts.

So what are the facts about the consequences of premarital sexual behavior—particularly if it occurs during the teenage years?

We'll get into some of the specific details of what a young boy has to lose by having a serious sexual relationship while he is still in high school, but here let's consider three general observations. First, there are problems regarding teenage sex—problems The Pill can't solve. Too many teenagers today have wrongly assumed that pregnancy is the only possible undesirable consequence of sex outside marriage, and, therefore, that in an era of sophisticated contraception, premarital sex was suddenly problem-free. As you'll see in the following sections, pregnancy is *still* a problem—but, as was always the case, it is not the *only* problem that can present itself. Second, probably the most important general adverse impact a teenage sexual relationship can have on a young man is that is has the potential to divert him from his most important "teenage business," the preparation for manhood and its responsibilities as a provider. We'll go more into the specifics of this later, but you should remember that, even in these days of women's liberation, it is the man who has the ultimate responsibility as the family breadwinner. It is he who will have to support himself, and probably a wife and family too. It is during his teenage years that a young man develops the type of maturity and skills that will allow him to perform this role.

Third, we should at least briefly comment on the age-old belief that "boys do not suffer consequences of sexual relationships. It's only the girl who has something to lose." This is the so-called "double standard" (we'll talk more about this in Chapter 8). But as Dr. Max Levin put it, "Boys *do* have a great deal to lose. The question is how to tell them that."

Maybe we could begin by telling you some of the more obvious problems that can occur in a teenage sexual relationship—and then turn to some of those problems with which you may not be as familiar.

THE UNINVITED BABY

Unwanted pregnancies in the Age of The Pill? Unfortunately, the answer is yes. And obvious though it is, it is worthwhile to point out that for every unwed prospective mother there is an unwed (at least to her) expectant father.

It is true that, as with most of the unexpected and undesired consequences of early sex relationships, the greater portion of the burden of the pregnancy falls on the girl. But not all of it does. If a man learns that he is a prospective father, he does not say, "Well, that's your problem." The developing life is just as much a part of him as it is of her. And he does not react casually to the diagnosis of his girlfriend's pregnancy. A study of a group of unwed fathers in Los Angeles found that most of them were totally shocked at the whole idea and initially rejected the announcement that they were prospective fathers. One boy just said, "It's impossible! We were just not having sex that often!" Another stunned boy exclaimed, "You're kidding! I am only sixteen! I'm not old enough to be a father!"

But of course they eventually had to accept the fact that a pregnancy had occurred—and that they *were* involved. Now what were they going to do about it? Yes, given our new abortion laws, the girl could terminate the pregnancy and the boy would cover her medical expenses. But maybe she didn't want to have an abortion. Maybe she thought abortion was immoral, and she fully intended to have the baby. And perhaps she would then exert pressure on the boy to marry her to "legitimate" the pregnancy.

The problem here, of course, is that the great majority of teenage boys are not emotionally or economically prepared to be husbands and fathers. And they find themselves being pressured unwillingly into a "shotgun marriage"; a wedding that is hurriedly arranged after a pregnancy is discovered. It is not uncommon for the boy who "has to get married" to live with a nagging question, "Am I sure this is *my* baby? Maybe there was another man in her life . . ."

It has been said that a teenage girl who conceives out of wedlock has, at that point, 90 percent of her life script written out for her. Her alternatives are few. She can have the baby and face the higher probability of all types of health risks that accompany early motherhood. She can get married and face the very high probability of divorce, which often is associated with a shotgun marriage. If she has the child, she will probably drop out of school and find that the responsibilities of parenthood are such that she never returns. Or she may have the child and offer it for adoption, or have an abortion.

But many of these problems can affect the unwed father as well. Often 90 percent of *his* life script may also have been written after the pregnancy is diagnosed. He too may have to drop out of school in order to assume his new economic responsibilities. He may suddenly find that he has to support a wife and child before he has had the opportunity to fully prepare himself for any job. And the effect that this premarital pregnancy—and the associated impact it has on his life—does not just disappear after a few years.

A well-known follow-up study of Detroit couples who "had to get married" because of a pregnancy found that these couples, as compared to those whose first baby was conceived in marriage, had significantly lower incomes *at every stage in their lives.* As the authors of this study put it, "Having a child . . . early [in marriage] is associated with distinct economic disadvantage, but if the child is conceived premaritally, this disadvantage is much greater than would be expected if the additional few months before having a child were all that were involved." And how are these results explained? The most obvious explanation, one that also was shown in this study, was that husbands who marry because of a pregnancy have less education and poorer economic potential.

But, you say, the problem is not really that dramatic because given the availability of contraception today, pregnancy just does not happen that often. Unfortunately, this is not true. Fully three out of every ten unmarried, sexually active teenage girls become pregnant. In a recent year some 640,000 women under the age of twenty had babies.

Looking at these figures from another point of view, it is evident that:

TWO of every one hundred girls have a baby by age sixteen.
FOUR of every one hundred girls have a baby by age seventeen.
NINE of every one hundred girls have a baby by age eighteen.
SEVENTEEN of every one hundred girls have a baby by age nineteen.
TWENTY-SIX of every one hundred girls have a baby by age twenty.

It is, of course, necessary to say "have babies" because an unknown number of teenage women had abortions. Official statistics on the incidence of abortion by age are not available, but in a recent year in New York City, there was one resident teenage abortion for every two resident teenage live births.

Think of the girls you know at school. If they are an average group of American women, and follow the same pattern as their older sisters, nearly a fifth of them will be mothers as they leave their teenage years, and an additional portion of the others may have had a pregnancy ended by abortion. So there goes the "Oh, she won't get pregnant" rationalization to which many teenage boys resort.

BUT WHY?

It doesn't seem to make sense that these pregnancies occur despite the availability of modern contraception. The Los Angeles study of unwed fathers showed that the young men knew about contraceptives and where to get them. But they decided not to use them, often because they thought birth control would make sex "less sincere," or because "they just forgot." Perhaps some of them simply felt that contraception was the girl's responsibility, and just assumed she was "on The Pill."

Psychiatrists who have looked into this problem have concluded that teenagers are not effective users of birth control. When you think about it, this makes sense. Most teens who are sexually active are not having regular intercourse. It happens on the spur of the moment, without any preparation. As pointed out by Dr. Frank J. Ayd, a psychiatrist who has written extensively about the problems of teenage sex, "Teenagers cannot be expected to use contraceptives intelligently or consistently." Indeed many of them do not use any type of birth control because they are unable or unwilling to acknowledge their behavior. In retrospect, they say they intended to have unprotected sex "just once" and they didn't think pregnancy could happen so quickly.

There is another point that you should consider. Avoiding pregnancy, even for adults, can be a very complicated matter! What a man or a woman *says* about a desire to avoid pregnancy may be very different from what he or she does. For instance, a teenage girl may tell her boyfriend she is taking The Pill, when indeed she isn't. Maybe she *wants* to become pregnant as a means, for instance, of forcing her boyfriend into marriage. It can work the other way too. Boys who convince a girl to have sexual intercourse may unconsciously hope that she becomes pregnant so that they can prove their manhood. Obviously, these are not healthy reasons for becoming parents. But they are still there.

So despite what you may hear to the contrary, teenage sexual relationships still carry with them very real risks of unwanted pregnancy and all the undesirable consequences that go with it. As summarized by Helen Colton, author of *Our Sexual Evolution*, we have "not yet achieved a way to save a young man or woman from the psychological pain of creating an unwanted human being. No other act in one's lifetime carries as heavy a burden of responsibility as the sex act."

DISEASE

You've undoubtedly heard of VD, the abbreviation for venereal disease, a category of several types of diseases, including syphilis and gonorrhea, which have a number of important things in common. Most important, they are passed from person to person by sexual contact. It's unfortunate that we even have to include disease in our discussion of sex. But we do, since today many people are misusing their sexuality, and disease is a possibility.

The history of venereal disease is a fascinating and thought-provoking one. One of the most common questions people first learning about the disease ask is, "Where did it come from in the first place? Has venereal disease always been around?"

An Ancient Problem

Medical historians have established that syphilis (and possibly some of the other venereal diseases) has been part of human life for centuries and may indeed date back to the beginning of the human race. Throughout history, plagues of syphilis have been responsible for crippling, blinding, bringing about insanity—and eventually killing millions of people.

And that means *all types* of people, even those who were wealthy and well respected. Careful investigations have shown that the famous Egyptian Pharaoh, Rameses V, had syphilis. Indeed, he may have been born with it.

The Greek physician, Hippocrates, in 460 B.C., and a Roman doctor in A.D. 25 described what seemed to be syphilis. But the real syphilis epidemic did not appear in Europe until the beginning of the sixteenth century. Why then?

Many historians believe that Christopher Columbus and his crew became infected with a highly infectious form of syphilis after having contact with the natives in the West Indies and took it back with them to Europe in 1493. Then, after the syphilis germs were introduced into European society, two important things happened. First, the period of the Renaissance took hold. People began to question former traditions and morality and sexual liberation became the theme. During this period, the moral code that previously had limited sex to marriage was temporarily broken down. Men began to have "many women," wives, slaves, and mistresses. Second, also about this time, men began to travel to new and previously unexplored parts of the world. They sought gold, spices, and other rare commodities in order to expand trade and commerce.

By means of the breakdown of sexual morals and the increased tendency to travel, the syphilis germ, introduced late in the 1400s spread like wildfire. A Spanish physician wrote that Columbus' associate, Martin Alonzo Pinzon, whose family had provided both the *Pinta* and *Niña*, and who had commanded the *Pinta*, caught syphilis on the first voyage and died from it after about two years. Many historians now also believe that Columbus himself caught the disease and became insane, dying fourteen years later.

About this time there were all types of names for syphilis—and it was inaccurately assumed that syphilis and gonorrhea were different stages of the same disease. The French called it the Neapolitan disease, because the first reported epidemic was in Naples. The Russians called it the Polish disease. The Persians called it the French disease. Others simply referred to it as "the great pox" (as opposed to smallpox) or "the evil pox." (It was in 1530 that an Italian doctor wrote a poem describing the disease as it affected a young shepherd boy named Syphilus, and thereafter syphilis became the official name for the disease.) But by whatever name they called it, all Europeans who had come into contact with it themselves, or knew of one of its victims, knew that it was a true scourge.

But let's now turn away from the history of these diseases, and focus on what they are and what they have in common.

Both syphilis (still known as "the pox" or "bad blood" or "the siff") and gonorrhea (also commonly known as "the clap") are transmitted through sexual contact. People used to believe that you could get VD from toilet seats, drinking cups, and even door-knobs in public places. But these were myths. Both of these forms of VD are primarily transmitted through sexual intercourse, although in unusual cases the disease can be passed from person to person through other types of contact with sexual organs and, in rare cases, through kissing if a person has an infectious VD sore on or around the mouth. The "toilet-seat theory" is ridiculous, because VD germs cannot survive for very long outside a warm, moist environment. They do, however, survive very well in a man's or woman's body.

Syphilis and gonorrhea have another thing in common. They both make life pretty miserable for the person who is unfortunate enough to be affected by them. Consider, for instance, the symptoms of gonorrhea, which is the most prevalent of the venereal diseases.

Gonorrhea

A man who has this disease may first notice pain during urination and possibly some secretion of pus from his penis. But this is in the man. Because of her different anatomy, the woman may not notice these first signs at all. Indeed gonorrhea may go right to work inside her body, and she might be totally unaware.

Any person who suspects that he or she might have gonorrhea should see a physician as soon as possible. But not all young people know enough to do so. Indeed, as was just mentioned, the girl may not even *know* she should go to a physician. In these cases, the boy and girl simply spread the disease to others with whom they have sexual contact. And they put themselves at the risk of becoming sterile—that is, gonorrhea in the male can affect the sperm duct in a way that emission of sperm becomes impossible. In the woman, untreated gonorrhea can result in complete or partial blockage of her fallopian tubes, potentially making it impossible for an egg to make its journey to the uterus. Untreated gonorrhea in both sexes may lead to a form of heart disease and gonococcal arthritis.

Syphilis

Now let's look at syphilis, a particularly lethal—and tricky—disease. You should recall here that syphilis is not in any way related to gonorrhea. The only thing they have in common is that they are both venereal diseases. But until the nineteenth century, people thought that they were the same disease. In 1767, some doctors began to suspect that they weren't the same, so Dr. John Hunter, one of England's most famous doctors, decided to settle this question once and for all. He infected himself with the pus from the discharge of a gonorrhea patient, and in time, he developed both the symptoms of syphilis and gonorrhea, and announced to the world that these were the same disease. But he had made a mistake. He didn't know that the patient he was working with and whose discharge he had used on himself had *both* gonorrhea and syphilis!

Some seventy years later, the discrepancy was corrected, and the symptoms of gonorrhea and syphilis were distinguished.

The organism that causes syphilis is *Treponema pallidum*. Once this lethal germ enters a person's body, it quietly goes about its work and is unnoticed by its victim. Then, after some ten to ninety days, the first stage of syphilis, *primary syphilis*, may be noticed. The first sign usually is a sore, called a "chancre," which generally appears where the syphilis germs first entered the body, on the lips, tongue or sex organs. This sore is usually painless, and feels something like a button under the skin. As was the case with gonorrhea, this first sign of syphilis is usually more noticeable in the man, as it appears on his penis. In the woman, the chancre may occur on her external genitalia, or in her vagina or cervix. In these latter cases, there would rarely be some outward signs. Because of this, a woman is often unaware of her primary syphilis, a condition that poses a particular risk to her sex partners.

If the infected person does nothing about the signs of primary syphilis, the sore will eventually heal. And this is how the disease is tricky. Instead of leaving the body, these germs "go into hiding" before the next and much more serious phase, *secondary syphilis.*

The most common signs of secondary syphilis are skin rashes, blotches, and bumps on any part of the body. The victim also may have a low fever, pain, headaches and not feel well. If not treated, these symptoms subside and the body may head toward *latent syphilis*, where usually no symptoms are noticeable, but the disease continues to ravage the body, attacking the brain, heart and other organs. The victim may be unaware of this damage until too late.

You may have heard of another type of syphilis, called *congenital syphilis*. If a mother has the disease while she is pregnant, she may very well transmit the germs to the baby growing inside her, and an innocent child may be born with a number of serious deformities, including advanced eye disease, which may end in blindness. (Henry VIII's daughter by Catherine of Aragon, Mary, or as she was known, "Bloody Mary," was born with syphilis; her face was deformed, and she was almost blind.)

Gonorrhea and syphilis are not pleasant to think about, and they should be avoided at all costs. But how does one avoid them, and what do people do when they do contract these diseases?

PREVENTION

The most obvious way to avoid venereal diseases is to avoid contact with an infected person. But for the unmarried boy or girl who is having sexual intercourse, this is not always easy to do.

Both forms of venereal disease spread easily. A boy may very easily pick up the infection from a girl who doesn't even know she has it. Some men do use condoms for protection, to lower the odds on either being infected with or transmitting venereal disease germs, but VD can be a consequence of sexual behavior.

A married couple generally does not have to worry about this problem. Before they are married, they have a blood test for syphilis (the Wasserman Test). A positive Wasserman *usually* means that a person has syphilis and a negative one means either that he does not or, in rare cases, that the disease is still in such an early stage it can't be detected. So generally, once a man and woman have been "cleared" in this fashion, and as long as their sexual contacts after the marriage are only with each other, there is generally no way for venereal disease germs to enter the body.

TREATMENT

People who do visit a doctor with symptoms of venereal disease are usually treated with penicillin (this is certainly more effective than the treatment of centuries ago, which involved giving the patients heavy doses of mercury, the silvery metal that looks like a liquid, and telling him to spit out at least three pints of saliva each day). Today's treatment is generally quick and effective (if the patient visits a doctor for help as soon as he or she notices symptoms). But even now there remains the possibility that VD germs eventually can build up resistance to penicillin, and the conclusion remains that venereal disease should be avoided at all costs.

PREMATURE SEX AND CERVICAL CANCER

There is another fact with which you should be familiar. Statistics have shown that girls who begin to have sexual intercourse early in their lives (for instance, before they are age sixteen) are twice as likely to develop cancer of the cervix than are girls who delay intercourse until later (until some time in their twenties). Exactly why youthful sex increases the chances of developing this form of cancer is uncertain. It has been suggested, however, that some of the sexual organs of girls who are not fully mature are more susceptible to whatever the cervical cancer-causing agent is.

BEYOND PREGNANCY AND DISEASE

At a lecture given by a physician-sex educator at a large urban high school, a student asked, "But, Doctor, what if someone invented a 'super pill,' which was guaranteed to prevent pregnancy *and* venereal disease without any medical side effects? What *then* would be wrong about having sex during your teen years?"

We've been focusing so far only on two of the most obvious consequences of premature sexual relations—pregnancy and disease. But there are other factors to be considered. And the next chapter will tell you all about them.

chapter 8

The Don Juan Myths

DON JUAN AND "SOWING YOUR OATS"

Don Juan is a legendary character who appears in the folklore of many European countries. Perhaps you've already read something about him in plays, poems, or operas. He is generally portrayed as a dashing, adventurous, reckless, arrogant young man—and women he encounters find him totally irresistible. He is a "lady's man" and is driven by a powerful urge to seduce one woman after another. As soon as the seduction of one woman is complete, he immediately moves on to another. He appears as a man totally devoid of moral principles, but he seems to get away with it. Indeed, many men throughout history have looked on the Don Juan character as a hero, a person who seems to be a triumph of sensuality, enjoying a colorful and fun-filled life without suffering any of the adverse consequences that can accompany the promiscuous use of sex.

This is how Don Juan appears on the *surface*. But some medical scientists, including Dr. Ira Miller, an associate professor of psychiatry at the University of Michigan, have taken the time to delve more deeply into what has come to be known as "the Don Juan syndrome"—that is, a man's preoccupation with seducing one woman after the other. And what Dr. Miller and others have found is very different from the superficial appearance that daring young hero seems to project. The Don Juan type, instead of receiving satisfaction from his many sexual exploits, feels nothing but frustration. As Dr. Miller notes, "After the sexual relationship is consummated, the Don Juan character feels strangely disappointed. The relationship has not provided him with a release from inner tensions. . . . He is to be more pitied than admired. . . . While he has matured physically as a man, he has remained a child emotionally." These young (or older) men are unable to relate emotionally to a woman—and if they begin to notice any personal involvement, they back away. This observation has provided evidence for the ancient saying about Don Juan-type men, "A thousand women are not enough, but one is too many."

You probably know of some people of both sexes who have come to be known as "Don Juan types" or "easy girls." All medical evidence supports the view that these individuals are truly pathetic, troubled by deep feelings of insecurity, inadequacy, and loneliness. A girl who moves from lover to lover may be trying to seek the type of love she never had at home. A boy who does so may be attempting to "prove he is a man." Some psychiatrists think that the promiscuous boy is actually afraid he is a homosexual (we'll read about that subject later in the chapter) and is trying to cope with this fear by identifying with Don Juan.

But of course, here we are talking about promiscuous individuals, those who have one sexual affair after the other. Some teenagers who are trying to defend the right of premarital sex say that having sexual intercourse with one or two special individuals early in the teenage years is not "permissive" or "promiscuous." But their conclusion is not valid in most of these cases because only the most unusual boy or girl who has had sexual intercourse in one relationship would revert to other forms of sexual expression with those they date later in their teenage life. And soon they find themselves falling into a pattern of behavior that, by anyone's standard, is permissive.

MYTHS ABOUT PREMARITAL SEX

The basic Don Juan myth has generated some widespread and related mini-myths, all of which claim to justify a boy's "right" to premarital sex. Let's take a look at seven of the most commonly raised myths.

"Girls Should Be Virgins, but Boys Will Be Boys" Myth

This is another name for the old double-standard myth, which is that boys should sow their oats while they are young, and then, when they start to think about settling down in marriage, should begin to look for a girl who is not sexually experienced.

This idea of a double standard with regard to sexual behavior can be traced back to the Bible, in which one passage states that a nonvirginal bride should be stoned, and no such statement is made for the boy. Similarly, a Roman code maintained, "If you [find] your wife in adultery, you may freely kill her without a trial. But if you commit adultery or if another commits adultery with you, she has no right to raise a finger against you."

But the fact that the double standard has been with us since earliest times does not make it right. As a matter of fact, the whole idea doesn't make sense at all.

If girls are to be virgins when they are married, and boys supposed to be "experienced," with whom are they supposed to sow their oats? The situation becomes even more ludicrous when exceptions are introduced into the double standard. A boy may claim that it is his right to sleep with any girl who is cooperative. But when it comes to discussing his sister and her potential sexual activity, he is very protective and indeed indignant if any young man "tries to mess around" with her. The same paradoxical situation may often occur with the father of a teenage daughter. A cartoon in *Parents' Magazine* once showed an obviously concerned father pacing the living-room floor at midnight one Saturday. His wife said, "Go to sleep, dear, and don't worry. Can't you remember when you were a teenager?" The husband said, "Yes, I can remember, and that's why I am worried!"

What he did when he was young was one thing. What the young men now might do with his daughter was another.

So our first myth is just that—an assumption that has no basis in fact. And boys who insist on operating under this double-standard assumption may find that they will encounter problems in later life. As summarized by Dr. Frances K. Harding, a physician at Ohio State University College of Medicine, "The devotee of the double standard cannot expect his eventual marriage to be the best and most enduring of all possible relationships if previously his relationships have been exclusively physical and transient."

"With The Pill, No One Will Get Hurt" Myth

Does this sound familiar? This is the myth the boy was operating under when he asked if, when a super pill was developed to guard against both pregnancy and verereal disease, teenage sex would be acceptable. He assumed that the possibility of pregnancy and venereal disease were the only deterrents to early sexual liaisons.

But he was misinformed. There are some other serious problems that have been linked with the irresponsible use of sex. Too often young boys find out about these other problems too late, and they can only wistfully say, "If I had only known then what I know today."

Sexual relationships can be the most constructive, liberating, and enriching of human experiences. But they can also be frustrating, destructive, and confusing if, as so often happens in a teenage relationship, sex is misused. Traditionally, it has been the belief that it is always the boy who "leads on the girl," and when the relationship is over that it is only she who will be emotionally devastated. But this has changed. With the availability of contraception—particularly The Pill—and a new sense of so-called "liberation," more *girls* are taking on the role of the seducers. Today, physicians point out, sexually involved teenagers of *both* sexes face the emotional trauma that can go with an unsuccessful experience.

You can see how a sexual relationship that develops outside of a context of love and security can lead to emotional problems. Sexual intercourse usually is accompanied by a wide range of deep, personal feelings. Whether these feelings add up to love or not, a couple who decides to have an intimate sexual relationship make a strong commitment to each other and develop a significant amount of dependence on each other. One or both of them assume that his or her "steady" is playing for keeps. But then a breakup occurs. Maybe the girl decides that she would like to move on and begin a relationship with one of his friends. Maybe the boy becomes concerned over the girl's frequent reference to "our future together." Or maybe both of them are going their separate ways after high school.

The type of heartbreak that goes with the termination of any serious romance is very real—even without the sex factor. But when you add the commitment that goes with the decision to have sexual intercourse—particularly when it is for the first time—the breakup brings with it unusually devastating emotional effects. People will continue to tell you that "boys don't get hurt by sexual involvements." But don't believe them. Many young men—and some older ones too—have been deeply and permanently affected by an unsuccessful sexual experience.

The "nobody is going to get hurt" myth overlooks the booby trap that accompanies it. A couple cannot *know* in advance that nobody is going to get hurt. They cannot predict that one of them will find a new interest a month or so after the affair begins. They cannot predict a pregnancy or a case of venereal disease and the associated trauma that go with these events. And they cannot know in advance what emotional impact their action is going to have on other people—their parents, for instance. They don't consider how a mother and father feel when they learn their daughter is pregnant, or that their son has syphilis, or when they see their child deeply depressed as a result of an unhappy sexual experience.

"Boys Need Experience To Be Good Husbands" Myth

This myth permits the assumption that sexual intercourse is like tennis, golf, or swimming, and that you need to practice it to be proficient. It also suggests that, if the man is not familiar with the logistics of sex, when he is married he will not be able to show his wife what sex is all about.

But of course, neither of the premises of this myth makes sense. Sexual intercourse techniques are not improved by practice with many women, and married couples with no experience learn very quickly together. To the contrary, there is some evidence that sexual experience before marriage may *interfere* with a man's potential to be a good husband, in that frequent and unsatisfactory premarital experiences and the guilt feelings and emotional trauma that may be associated with them may leave him with some very poor attitudes.

Studies have shown that teenagers very often enter their first sexual union with high hopes—and emerge depressed with a set of unmet expectations. The study of unwed fathers (most of whom admitted that they chose to have intercourse as a means of "proving their manhood") found that many boys reported that "the good relationships they had with their girlfriends began to deteriorate when they began to have sexual intercourse." These young men further stated that intercourse proved to be "hardly the glamorous experience they had been led to expect. It was often disappointing, disillusioning, and depressing."

This type of initiation into sex—when combined with the emotional hangover that may follow the termination of the relationship—hardly provides the type of background that would lead to healthy sexual adjustment in marriage.

You may be wondering *why* these young boys were so disappointed in sex. How would it be different for them if they were older and married?

There are at least two differences between the sexual activity of a young unmarried teenager and older married adults. First, the "give element" is often missing. The type of love and devotion that bind a man and woman together in marriage and in their sexual relationship is based on a complete willingness to *give* emotional and physical satisfaction as well as receive it. Indeed, it is often *more* important in a mature relationship to be more concerned about the other individual and her need than you are about your own. But outside marriage, especially when a boy and girl are young, the motivation is often different. Sex may be more of an experiment—to "see what we can get out of it." It is not a mature giving relationship.

Second, these two types of relationships are distinguishable because they occur in different circumstances. Premarital sex may take place in a hurried fashion in odd places—and usually quite irregularly. There is, even among the most "liberated" of couples, a distinct feeling of guilt and often a concern that "someone might find out" or "we might be caught." Now compare this to a marriage situation, in which there is no guilt about sexual intercourse, there is a feeling of serenity and security, and sex is more regular and predictable. One situation is conducive to good sexual relations, the other isn't.

But you'll still keep hearing about the "have sex and prepare for marriage" myth. And some of your friends even may try to convince you that you shouldn't get married at all until you have had intercourse with a girl. It will be easy for them to draw analogies, pointing out that you certainly would not think of buying a car without a test run. But don't fall for their "reasoning." As psychiatrist Dr. Max Levin pointed out, "The test of sexual compatibility is too important to be undertaken under anything less than the most favorable conditions. This optimal condition is not premarital intercourse with its room for mistrust."

Indeed there is some evidence that the premarital sexual-compatibility test often yields false positives—that is, it leads couples to assume that they will have a well-adjusted sex life when they get married. But then, after the ceremony, they run into problems. The illicit factor and guilt feeling are gone. For them, the sexual relationship has lost the glamour that some people associate with forbidden things and behavior. They find that their plan has backfired on them and the love and sensuality that might, under other circumstances, be part of their marriage is not there.

During your teen years you can prepare to be a good husband (that is, if you choose to be married at all). But working at sexual experience is not the wisest route to follow. The best type of preparation you might make is the exercise of self-restraint. You can even think of it in economic terms—as an investment. The cost of this "policy"—that is, of depriving yourself of sexual opportunities—may be high now, but it will yield great dividends later. You—unlike some of your Don Juan–type associates—will have an excellent chance for a stable and rewarding marriage, if you choose it.

"If You Are in Love, It's Okay" Myth

There are at least two problems here. First, love is a complex and basically unselfish emotion. Eric Fromm, author of *The Art of Loving,* tried to identify exactly what goes into "true love" and he concluded that it involved four essential components: the willingness to work for your loved one, a strong feeling of responsibility for him or her, an attitude of respect, and a pervasive feeling of understanding. Basically, love requires that two people are willing and able to make sacrifices for each other. And that type of feeling and capacity takes time. It is not suddenly there when a young adult becomes physically mature. If a boy and girl really are in love, they certainly would not ask each other to assume the risks that go with teenage sex. Besides, if they actually *did* plan to get married, they would have all the more reason to postpone intercourse until a time and place where they could feel certain that this important phase of their married life was beginning under the best of conditions.

Second, marriage, unlike a premarital love affair, involves a total, lifetime commitment. The formal wedding ceremony solemnizes that commitment. And that cannot be taken lightly. It is *not* a commitment for a boy and girl to say, "We are in love, let's have sexual relations" or "You turn me on." They are not formally assuming the responsibility for the consequences that may accompany their actions.

"Sex Is Natural, You Need It To Stay Healthy" Myth

The idea that sexual intercourse is natural and is indeed "good for you" as soon as a boy matures is based on two assumptions, both of which misinterpret the basic facts.

First, people who use this argument will try to convince you that once a young man begins to have seminal emissions he will be injuring his health by not having intercourse. Of course, this is ridiculous. Sperm are naturally released from a man's body as they are produced—either in wet dreams, through masturbation, or gradually in the urine. Sexual intercourse is *not* necessary and in most cases is not desirable at all.

Second, there is nothing at all unhealthy about controlling physical impulses. People who have heard about Sigmund Freud—or possibly have read some of his works—often conclude that he recommended dropping all restraints on behavior. But he advised no such thing. When Freud wrote about "repressed" feelings and their potential for causing mental distress, he was referring to *unconscious* feelings. For instance, he reported that some of his adult patients had repressed some very natural fantasies and curiosities about sex during their infancy and childhood. These repressed thoughts may have had undesirable effects on their later sexual attitudes. But he certainly did not suggest that we abandon *conscious* restraints and do everything we want to.

Our life is full of conscious restraints. After high school, for instance, you might have a strong desire to "take off" and travel around the world instead of continuing your studies at college or in a career-training course. And certainly that would be fun. But you probably would restrain this urge in favor of planning for your future. This is conscious repression, and you will be benefiting from it.

"A Boy Can't Be a Man Until He Has Sex" Myth

This fallacy is based on the theme that "a healthy red-blooded man needs a woman," and ignores the more basic observation that a *really* healthy red-blooded man has self-control and a genuine desire to postpone sex until a time in his life when he can really enjoy it and can accept all the consequences that may go with it.

But still this myth is perpetuated. Somehow in recent years, some teenagers have become convinced that sex becomes natural as soon as a man physically grows up, and that he should be "initiated" as soon as possible. After some of the potential problems you already have read about, you can see why this route to "becoming a man" is hardly very effective. Indeed, by becoming sexually involved, many young men—and young women— forgo many of the opportunities that *would* contribute to their maturity and self-confidence.

Growing up means having the opportunity to meet and get to know all types of individuals—male and female, young and old. You should constantly be meeting people—and constantly learning from them. As you probably have noticed so far in your teenage life, each individual with whom you come into contact—at school, in your neighborhood, in sports activities, in dating—is unique in his or her own way. And you pick up new information and new ideas from him or her. It is *important* that you get accustomed to dealing with people. It helps you to understand yourself and where you are going in life.

But the boy and girl who enter into a serious sexual relationship lose sight of the people around them. They limit the number of friends they have and they usually choose not to date others. They even may find out that their relationships with their brothers, sisters, and parents begin to deteriorate. And this sense of "exclusiveness" can have an adverse effect on their emotional and social development. As pointed out by Dr. Samuel S. Kaufman, a New York psychiatrist, one real tragedy of the sexual revolution is that it robs young people of their opportunity for psychological growth. A boy and girl having sex while they are still in high school are not growing in his or her "own" direction.

Psychologists studying the impact that irresponsible use of sexuality can have on personality development have concluded that young adults who enter into premature relationships often suffer in terms of emotional stability and personality development. Researchers have noted that teenagers who trust themselves, who contribute to others, and who can rely on others tend to have the least number of premarital sexual relationships. The well-known psychologist Abraham Maslow has described the personalities of "self-actualized" adults—that is, those who were highly successful in whatever work they chose, satisfied with their life and generally happy about their existence. He found that these individuals had fewer premarital contacts than less successful people. And additionally, they seemed to enjoy their mature sexual relationships more than did those who began to have intercourse earlier.

Your teenage years are a time of preparation for manhood. You will be turning twenty-one sooner than you think, and you want to be ready to accept the responsibilities and challenges that will present themselves. One type of preparation we have discussed already—the thinking ahead to the time you may decide to get married and have children. You *certainly* would not want to say "I do" until you had dated many different types of girls. But boys having sexual intercourse with their girlfriends often deny themselves this option. Sexually committed girls tend to be very possessive—and often very demanding. And this can certainly set limits on a young man's freedom to go where he wants and do what he knows is best for him.

But there is more than just the "marriage preparation" activity. While you are in high school, you will be making decisions and taking courses of action that will determine exactly what type of a man you will be. You will be thinking about what type of education or vocational training you would like to pursue after high school. And you will be working hard at school to make sure that, when graduation time comes, the options you have chosen are still available to you. You'll be thinking about a career commitment and generally what type of life you want to lead. You will be preparing yourself intellectually and emotionally to make a contribution to society and provide a source of income for yourself, and maybe for others as well. You'll be deriving a mature sense of self-direction, one that includes a sincere concern about the welfare of others. And *this* type of activity *proves* you are well on your way to manhood!

"Everyone Has Sex These Days, What's Wrong with You" Myth

Dr. Richard Lee, a physician at the Yale School of Medicine, has written a number of articles in which he explains how many of his male patients feel that they are inadequate or "strange" because they are not having sexual relations. They have been misled by the "everyone is doing it" claim. And this very much disturbs Dr. Lee, who refers to these men as casualties of a sexual ideology that is "as dictatorial and cruel as Victorian prudery."

This concern about "abnormality" on the behalf of boys who do not choose to have premarital sex has become particularly noticeable in recent years as girls become more sexually aggressive. As Dr. Seymour L. Halleck, a professor of psychiatry at the University of North Carolina, put it, "The boy who chooses to abstain . . . after being told that girls are more promiscuous than ever, feels more freakish than ever before. . . . For some students, such stresses have been critical facts in [bringing about] severe emotional disorders. . . . In this sense, a significant number of students are casualties of the sexual revolution."

The problem here is that these boys are responding to the pressures around them. They are forgetting (most of them just temporarily) that the standard for all human behavior is "do what *you* think is best, not what others are doing," and they become dropouts from themselves.

But you have the facts now, and *you* should make up your own mind and not be influenced by what those around you are doing. And, by the way, you shouldn't become convinced by that casual statement that everyone is doing it. We do not have statistics about what percentage of high-school-age boys are sexually active, but we can be confident that more boys *say* they are "experienced" (and brag about it) than is actually the case. We do have some estimates from national surveys on the extent of sexual experience in teenage unmarried women, and the statistics definitely confirm that everyone is *not* doing it. *Less than 28 percent* of teenage girls aged seventeen and younger reported that they have had sexual intercourse, and this may be an exaggeration of many of them who wanted to give the "in" answer and appear sophisticated.

SETTING YOUR LIMITS

Part of our new attitudes about sex and sexual behavior is that individual men and women must define for themselves their sexual code. And you will have to decide yours too! There are no firm answers to the "setting the limits" question, but there are a few things that you should know before you make any decision.

First, you should know that a teenage girl's attitude about sex may be very different from yours. While you might ask, "How far can I go?", her question is more likely to be, "How far is too far?"

For a girl, a session of relaxed kissing and caressing may be a pleasant, but not particularly sexually stimulating experience. She may just enjoy being "cuddled," while for you these types of activities may be particularly stimulating—and may provoke a desire for more intimate involvement. Girls—particularly when they are sexually inexperienced—do not become sexually aroused as quickly as boys. And sometimes they do not know the effect their actions are having. Many boys, in fact, complain that it is the girls who make it difficult to keep relationships on a nonphysical level. In extreme cases, some girls actually try to exploit—or cruelly tease—a boy by overstimulating him and then quickly "turning off."

But on the other extreme, a girl may passively respond to a boy's advances, not because she really wants to become sexually involved, but because she naively thinks that by "giving in" she is assuring herself the chance for more romance—and possibly even the chance for marriage. A well-informed young man will keep these "motivational differences" in mind when he is making decisions about sex.

Petting: Wise or Otherwise?

As you have probably figured out, there are various phases of intensity in a sexual relationship. Men and women do not go from simple kissing to having sexual intercourse. There is a progression of intimacy in between.

It is difficult to describe the various levels of sexual activity because people have different interpretations for words such as "necking," "making out," or "petting." Necking generally refers to physical contact that is, quite literally, limited to above the neck. But there can be differences here, too. Gentle caressing with light kissing is one thing. But intense kissing ("soul kissing," "French kissing," or whatever you call it) is something very different, something much more involved and sexually stimulating. Similarly, petting, which usually refers to sexual behavior that involves the caressing and fondling of the breasts or chest, the thighs, or direct contact with the sexual organs, leads to an even more advanced state of excitement.

When petting of this type takes place, the body of both the girl and boy respond quickly. There is a widening of the blood vessels, a warm blush that may cover the whole body, and a pervasive tingling sensation. The blood volume in the sexual organs is greatly increased. Quite simply, the bodies of the couples who are involved in this type of behavior are becoming fully prepared for sexual intercourse. And sometimes it is not so easy to turn off nature's processes. We said earlier that women usually take a longer period of time, and require more stimulation, before they become sexually aroused. But once they do, the desires for intercourse and orgasm are as strong as they are for a man. And aroused sexual feeling can be dynamite, and physical desire has been known to overrule rational concerns.

So you'll want to decide about your own sexual code *before* you find yourself in a romantic situation. You'll want to set your limit in a manner that allows the expression of natural affection without stimulating her body (or yours) to the point where sexual intercourse could occur in a moment of passion—without benefit of the rational consideration it merits.

HOMOSEXUALITY

These last two chapters have focused on questions related to sexual behavior between a man and a woman—that is, *heterosexual behavior*. A minority of men and women (about 4 percent of men and 2 percent of women) do not enjoy heterosexual activity, and seek sexual activity exclusively with members of their own sex. These people are called *homosexuals* (the woman is usually referred to as a *lesbian*).

It is really impossible to make sweeping statements about the "right" and "wrong" of homosexual feelings and experiences because there are so many levels on which they can occur. But let's start by considering the two extremes.

Psychiatrists feel strongly about their observation that *all* young men at some point in their teenage years have some type of homosexual attraction, minor though it may be. And this, they feel, is natural and normal. Some young boys still worry—about having a form of hero worship for a man in their life, or even having crushes of sorts on boys their age. But they shouldn't worry. Sometimes this interest in other boys and men extends to the point where boys explore each other's bodies. This is more a matter of curiosity than a source of concern, and doctors accept this feeling and interest as being a normal stage of male development.

But now let's look at the other extreme, a form of behavior that is definitely abnormal, and something of which young men should be aware.

Some small percentage of men—usually middle-aged or older men—actually enjoy sexually molesting teenage boys. Their seduction attempts may be somewhat unclear at first, but soon it becomes very evident that they are interested in getting the boy to participate in some type of homosexual activity. This is *not* normal, although it is certainly not unusual for an adolescent boy to experience at least one such incident.

Most boys have no trouble making the point that they are not interested, and the would-be seducer goes away. But occasionally, the problem can occur more than once with the same person and in this case the boy will want to report it to his parents and possibly to a law-enforcement agency.

There are those men, young and old, who are neither "youthful experimenters" nor "child molesters." They are just confirmed homosexuals, those who openly (or not so openly) admit that they prefer men to women in sexual encounters. By no stretch of the imagination can this behavior be categorized as "normal," and we do not really understand why it occurs. Most researchers who have studied this subject feel that the problem is more psychologically than physically based, and may stem from a poor family relationship during childhood.

But while homosexual activity cannot be called normal, at the same time it cannot rightly be labeled "a sickness that needs treatment." Some men do seek medical help, and undergo a form of psychotherapy in an attempt to alter their behavior. Others, however, accept that they are homosexuals and feel that they should not be prejudiced against because of their unusual interest in members of their own sex. And most people are beginning to accept the general principle that homosexuals of either sex—while their behavior cannot be regarded as normal—should not be considered as criminals or mentally disturbed individuals. If the two people involved are "consenting" adults, and do not attempt to seduce unwilling partners, their interests and behavior are only their own business.

SEX AND SENSE

As a teenager you'll be making a wide variety of important decisions—possibly among them, decisions about sex. Of course you will be thinking, learning, and deciding about sex throughout your whole life. But your actions during your high school years and early twenties are particularly important in that they can have such a major impact on the direction your life will take.

Making decisions about sex is a very complicated matter. The teen years for a boy are a time of maximal sexual drive. Your body very often will be saying "yes," even though your sense of reasoning is saying "no." Additionally, it is a time of your life when you will hear all points of view on the matter of sex and the role it should be playing in a teenage boy's life. You'll hear all the "myths" presented here and many more. And in the midst of all this confusion, you will have to decide. In making up your mind about your own personal code of sexual ethics, be guided by four principles.

First, make your decisions *before* you get into a romantic setting. After you are physically aroused, the circumstances are hardly ideal for rational decisions. Don't count on the girl to say "stop." She may have some ideas that are very different from yours.

Second, take into account all the facts you have read about in this book and those you will pick up elsewhere. You would never make any other important life decision without a complete set of facts, and this situation should be no different.

Third, do what *you* think is right, not what anyone else is suggesting "is the thing to do." Be your own person, and avoid the "going along with the gang" approach to life.

Fourth, make sure all your actions have an element of responsibility in them. Think about the obligations you may be assuming.

Think about the consequences that may stem from various types of behavior. Responsible decisions of all types require a full knowledge of the facts involved and a mature concern and respect for the impact that decision may have on others. Responsible decisions about sex specifically require a sincere commitment to avoid any behavior that could cause harm to yourself or any other human being—one already living, or one not yet born.

chapter 9

Where Are You Going In Life?

YOUR THREE BIGGEST DECISIONS

Try to think ahead to the time when you are five years and then ten years older than you are now. What do you imagine your life will be like then? Do you think you will still be in school—either college or graduate school? Do you think perhaps you will be working at a full-time job? What will your family life be like? Do you imagine yourself as being married, and possibly the father of some children? Or do you consider yourself to be more of the "bachelor type" (at least for a few years)?

It is useful to think ahead like this. Of course, you can never be sure what the future will bring, but by considering seriously what you expect your life to be like, you can begin to formulate your own personal goals—and you can start to take steps that will increase your chances of reaching these goals. You might think of life as a series of "climbs" aimed at reaching different levels, or plateaus. Right now you are on one plateau, but you are already looking ahead and planning for the next. If you are in your teen years right now, you are probably asking yourself, "Where do I want to be at age twenty-one?" And when you reach age twenty-one, you will have a new plateau in mind, possibly thinking, "Where do I want to be when I am thirty?" Life is a series of learning experiences. We are *always* learning and very often modifying our goals as we move on in life. And speaking of plateaus, and climbing, we might learn a lesson from professional mountain climbers and their strategy for success. They don't just set out one day and decide they are going to "climb the mountain." They approach this challenge slowly—gradually. They spend some time on each plateau to get used to it, to become accustomed to the air pressure, for instance. They wouldn't make it if they didn't take this caution. Life isn't very much different from that. We've got to learn to understand one stage of life before we can move on to the next. And this applies to the "plateau" of young adulthood. This plateau is one of preparation. People who rush through it in eager anticipation of the "mature adult plateau" just above it often find that when they get there they can't cope.

From now on, you will be continuously making decisions, many of which will have dramatic effects on the direction your life will take. But three of these decisions stand out as being extra important. And chances are you already know what they are: (1) your choice of a career, (2) your decision about the "if, when and who" of marriage, and eventually, (3) the "if, when and how many" of parenthood.

Choosing Your Life's Work

You may be somewhat surprised that a book entitled *Making Sense Out of Sex* has even a brief discussion about choosing a career and thinking ahead to the time when you will be a self-supporting independent man. After all, in the earlier chapters we were concerned only with the reproductive facts of life and information necessary for making intelligent decisions about sexual behavior. So where does career planning come in?

Actually, some consideration of your life plan and choosing a vocation are *very* much related to the topics of growing up and dealing with your feelings and awareness of sexuality. Too many young men become so distracted by an interest in sex that they forget what the teenage years are really all about. They forget that the number-one priority during their high school days is education and preparation for manhood (and the responsibilities that go with it). And as a result, they pass up educational and social opportunities that would help them mature in a manner that would contribute to their ability to get—and keep—the type of job that would be both economically and emotionally rewarding.

You certainly have a great deal of different activities planned for your life—and working at a job is only one of them. But let's project ahead again, just to put the "at work" portion of your life in perspective.

Let's assume this time that you are thirty years old. When you wake up on a Monday morning, what do you do? Unless you are independently wealthy, you get up and go to work. And you stay there for about eight hours—five days a week, probably on some two hundred and thirty days of every year, for at least forty years of your life! You will spend more time at your job than you will at any other type of life activity (except maybe sleeping)!

Unfortunately, however, not everybody is happy with the career they choose (or maybe they didn't choose it, it may have just happened). Often this is because a man either did not take the time to do some advance planning, or he didn't allow himself the necessary preparation that would allow him to do what he really would *like* to do. (Our emphasis here is on the man because, as we stressed before, he is still the major source of income, and the chances are that he will *have* to work.) Often these disillusioned people look back on their teenage years thinking, "If I had only known then what I know now, I would have had some different priorities in high school!"

You've undoubtedly been asked "What are you going to do when you grow up?" ever since the time you learned to talk! But now that question has more relevance than ever. It is a critical decision, one that most young men make in that all-important ten-year span between age fifteen and age twenty-five. Of course, some men are certain about their career plans even before age fifteen. And others may never finally make specific work plans by their mid-twenties. But the great majority of young men do come to grips with this question while they are in high school, and if they continue their education, while they are in college.

Maybe you are the unusual type who "always knew what he wanted to be." Maybe since childhood you wanted to be a musician, policeman, doctor, teacher, or lawyer. And you've already made up your mind, although, of course, you will be doing some constant "self-assessment" as you continue your education to make sure that decision is the right one. But if you are like most teenagers, you are still considering all your options—and you will make this decision very gradually.

The first option that will probably confront you while you are in high school concerns what you will do *after* high school. Will you go right to work? Will you enter some type of vocational school that will prepare you for the career of your choice? Will you go on to college? These are questions to start thinking about now so that in your remaining high-school years you can make sure that you are fully prepared to make the move you want. Then, once you've made the decision about immediate employment, vocational training, or college, you can get more specific about the direction your life will take. Do your interests lean toward science? Mechanical work? Social service? The arts?

Your high school may have some type of career-planning program in which you can learn what type of tasks and responsibilities are associated with various vocations. You even may have the opportunity to consult a guidance counselor. And certainly your parents will have some advice to offer. In the end, of course, only you will decide what type of work is best for you.

What About Marriage?

You probably think of marriage as being "way off in the future sometime." And if you are the typical American male, it will be. (The average American man marries at about age twenty-three.) Perhaps you don't think you will *ever* get married, and maybe you won't (although if your generation follows the trend set by your older brothers and fathers, there is over a 90 percent chance that you will marry). In any case, it is still not too early to at least *think* about marriage as a life option, and to consider when, if at all, you might say "I do."

The age of which a young man marries is to a great extent a matter of choice, and is very much influenced by the other goals he has in mind for himself. If you are going on to college—and perhaps for graduate training—you might not feel economically independent enough to support a wife even though you are twenty-three. You might delay a wedding until the time when you have a job and feel economically secure. On the other hand, if you had completed your training after high school and by age twenty-one had an established job, you might be ready for marriage then—that is, if the right young woman has presented herself.

But there are some factors about the timing of marriage that are not entirely in the realm of personal opinion. It has been shown that teenage marriages carry with them a higher-than-average probability of eventual divorce. This is particularly true when the bride or the groom, or both, are under age eighteen. If, for instance, a twenty-year-old boy marries a seventeen-year-old girl, they may find that within three or four years they have both become different people. The teenage years, and the early twenties, are times when personalities, attitudes, and outlooks on life can change dramatically. If marriage intervenes in these years of alteration, the boy may grow one way, and the girl the other. All of a sudden they may inhabit the same house, but their individual personalities and life styles could be in two different worlds.

On the other hand, the couples who marry when they are older, say in their middle or late twenties, have completed much of that transition. They have become relatively set in their ways and have been around long enough to know what they want and don't want in their lifelong partner. They are more mature and are capable of making more mature decisions than are most teenagers. These couples have a much lower divorce rate than do their friends who married earlier.

It has also been shown that the *motivation* behind the decision to get married can have an important influence on whether or not the marriage is successful.

Consider the ideal motivation for marriage: A mature man and woman acknowledge their mutual love and, without reacting from any outside pressure, decide to make a lifetime commitment to each other. Now think of another common, but less than ideal, circumstance for marriage: A young man and woman are dating, they become sexually involved, and a pregnancy is discovered. Then the pressure is on. Maybe this couple would have been married anyway, but maybe they would not have. They have denied themselves the opportunity to choose a marriage partner (the unborn baby may be the real decision maker).

In choosing the woman with whom you will share the rest of your life, you certainly do not want to be under pressure from an unborn baby or from any source at all. But unfortunately, a significant number of teenage marriages begin under these circumstances. Researchers studying the subject of premarital conception have found that almost half of first babies born to teenage girls are conceived before they marry. Among very young teenagers, the percentage having babies less than eight months after the wedding is almost 100 percent.

Will You Be a Parent?

If you do marry, at some point during your married life you'll want to consider the possibility of having children. Whatever your decision, you will want to think about it. Then, if you decide to do so, you'll have to do some more thinking about the "when" and "how many" of parenthood.

Throughout most of our history, couples did not give too much thought to the question of parenthood. It was just assumed that a baby would arrive within a year or so after the wedding, and that brothers and sisters would appear regularly after that. But things have changed dramatically. Today couples are thinking very carefully about the question "Do we want children at all?" And then, if they do decide "yes" (over 95 percent of couples still do), many choose to have small, well-planned families. Today we are faced with some facts that were unheard of in your grandparents'—even your parents'—days.

You probably can identify one obvious factor that has led to the trend toward smaller families, and in some cases the decision to have no children at all. The mechanisms of contraception we have today are highly sophisticated, and couples now have the opportunity to avoid unwanted pregnancy, and postpone wanted ones. But there are more than pills and devices involved in this trend. Modern couples have a new and realistic awareness about the impact children can have on their lives.

First, they know that having a baby—like everything else in our era of rising prices—is now very expensive.

Second, they know that raising a child requires a great deal of time and effort, particularly on the part of the wife. Many women now feel that while they do want to have children, they also want time for other activities. And by having a small family, they manage to have the time to pursue a career or some community activities.

Third, married couples today have a new social awareness about the problems of the so-called "population explosion." They are concerned about the effect that too many people could have on the quality of life on this planet. You are probably concerned about this too (if not, you should be). There are over 210 million Americans living right now. You may have read some things about "zero population growth" and how our country's birth rate is as low as it has ever been. But don't think that means that our population has now stopped growing. It certainly has not! The rate has just slowed down some—possibly only temporarily. We still add about two million people *each year* (that's just about the number of people living in the city of Philadelphia). It does not take a large percentage of growth to make a population expand quickly. For instance, what may sound like a low growth rate of 1 percent (our current growth rate is just under that) will *double* the population in seventy years!

Demographers (they are the scientists who count people, study and make projections about such subjects as births, deaths, marriages, and divorces) tell us that if women have an average of three or more children, our country's population growth rate will be a real source of concern. By the year 2000 (when you'll probably be around age forty), at the present rate there would be over 320 million Americans, and by the middle of the next century (when your grandchildren would be about your age now), there would be over 400 million! You can imagine what that would be like; we know how many problems we now have feeding, clothing, and supplying sources of energy for 210 million.

If, on the other hand, couples have an average of two children, the population would be more like 270 million by the year 2000—and that is still a great deal more people to deal with. But it would represent a significant slowdown in our rate of growth.

Some people say, "Oh, we don't have to worry about having too many people in the United States. We are a rich country, and we can solve any problem." But it is becoming increasingly evident that these people are unrealistically optimistic. Our gasoline shortages and general "energy crisis" showed us that pretty clearly. And there is another very important point here. Our country's growth rate is just one part of the worldwide problem. It is a well-established fact that our nation consumes far more than "our share" of natural resources. So, although our growth rate is not as high percentage-wise as that of some other countries, the impact that our expanding population can have on world supplies is particularly significant.

So when and if you marry, what would you do about "the population problem"? Obviously, one thing you could do is have a small family. But that *does not* mean that you must have "2.1 children" (that's the statistical average for zero population growth—that is, it allows a man and woman to replace themselves, and allows a slight margin for those women who die before they have any children. From the demographer's point of view, only women are significant in projecting population figures as only they will be actually producing the children). There are many ways for couples to have an average of two children. If, for instance, 25 percent of couples have no children at all, and 25 percent had one child, then another 25 percent could have three, and the final 25 percent four children.

Having children, and determining how many will be planned, is a very personal matter. We are not at the point (at least not yet) where we are told how many children we are "allowed." Instead, we have reached a point where we make this decision very carefully, taking into account a wide variety of factors, including the possibility of runaway growth rate. And *this* was something your parents and grandparents didn't think about at all.

Let's for a moment assume that you will become a father of one, two, or three children. When would be the best time to have them?

As was the case with the timing of marriage, planning the "when" of parenthood is generally a personal decision, one that is determined by other factors in your life. But you should be aware of two important considerations. First, there is evidence that having a child very soon after the marriage—even if that baby was conceived after the wedding ceremony—is linked with higher chances of divorce. It takes some time to become accustomed to being married. You certainly should know the woman you are going to marry pretty well before the wedding—but you will get to know her even better in the first few months of your life together. A husband and wife who don't give themselves time to adjust run into more than their share of problems. Additionally, marriage is a new and exciting way of life, and most couples want to get used to being just the "two of them" before they accept the responsiblities that go with being the "three of them." The most common interval between marriage and the first birth (that is, when the baby was conceived after the wedding) is somewhere in the one- to two-year range. The great majority of married couples who do plan to have children at all have their first within five years of their wedding date. But of course, those generalities need not affect your decision.

Second, the wife's age is often a consideration in planning parenthood. Physicians feel strongly that it is *not* a good idea for a woman to have a baby too early in life (say before age eighteen).

Nor is it a good idea to wait too long (for instance after thirty-five) to start a family. It is not good for the mother's health, or the baby's health.

Even without pregnancy, the second decade of life is characterized by increasing nutritional demands. Growing girls and boys require the right food. But for a woman, pregnancy brings with it additional nutritional demands—and a combination of these two circumstances of "extra needs" often leads to problems. A young mother's pregnancy and the actual childbirth process carry a higher-than-expected risk of complications. And her baby is more likely than a baby born to an older mother to weigh less when it is born and have a lower probability of surviving during its first year in life.

But that's one end of the age spectrum. You should also know that it is not a good idea to wait *too* long to have a baby. A woman's fertility—that is, her chances of becoming pregnant—may diminish after age thirty or thirty-five. Similarly, it is known that the probability of certain birth defects, for instance, *mongolism* (a condition in which the child is born with slanted eyes, a large tongue, a broad, short skull, and is generally severely retarded) is increased substantially after age thirty-five (the odds go from about one in 1,500–3,000 births in the ages under thirty to about one in 280 births if the mother is between thirty-five and thirty-nine).

But there is a great deal of leeway between the ages of twenty and thirty-five. And this is generally when couples do have their children.

DECISIONS BY CHOICE—NOT CHANCE

All your important decisions—whether they relate to a career choice, life priorities, sexual activity, marriage, or parenthood—should be made on both the basis of facts *and* responsible judgment. They should not "just happen."

These may initially appear to you to be unnecessarily obvious statements to make. But these observations are so important, they *should* be repeated. If you are going to get the most out of life and make your own unique contribution to solving some of the world's problems, you must take the "choice" approach to decision making, and avoid, at all costs, the "chance" route. During your teenage years, this particularly applies to your decisions about sexual activity, because these carry with them consequences that can drastically reduce the number of lifetime options still available to you when you reach twenty.

You've read about the complex process of reproduction, about the creative use of human sexuality, and about the problems that can occur if sex is misused. You have had a chance to think through some of your own personal priorities for your teenage years, and perhaps now you have begun to set some specific goals. You have the basic facts. You know how mature, responsible decisions are made. And now, it's up to you.

Words You'll
Want To Know

This glossary contains not only many of the words you read in this book, but also a number that were not mentioned.

ABORTION	Any interruption of pregnancy, either accidental (spontaneous) or induced.
ACIDIC	Sour, sharp or bitter, the opposite of alkaline.
ADOLESCENCE	The developmental period between puberty and the beginning of adulthood.
AFTERBIRTH	The placenta and other membranes associated with the fetus, expelled from the mother's body after childbirth.
ALKALINE	Having a salt base; the opposite of acidic.
AMENORRHEA	The failure to menstruate.
AMPULLA	The storage place (or "sperm reservoir") for sperm prior to ejaculation.
ANATOMY	The study of the structure of the human organism.
ANDROGEN	Any substance that stimulates male characteristics. Testosterone is an androgen.
ANUS	The opening through which solid wastes from the large intestine are released from the body.
AREOLA	The pigmented area around the nipple of the breast.
ARTIFICIAL INSEMINATION	The introduction of semen into the woman's vagina or cervical canal by artificial means.
BAG OF WATERS	A sac of fluid that protects the baby during pregnancy.

BARREN	See STERILE.
BARTHOLIN'S GLANDS	The glands located near the vagina, which produce mucous secretions to keep the vagina moist and lubricated.
BASAL BODY TEMPERATURE	The body-temperature reading obtained by using a special type of thermometer every morning upon awakening before engaging in any type of physical activity.
BIRTH CONTROL	Any means of controlling the number of live births.
BREASTS	The structures that in the female hold the mammary glands.
BULBO-URETHRAL GLANDS	See COWPER'S GLANDS.
CAESAREAN SECTION	The delivery of a baby by cutting through the mother's abdominal wall.
CALENDAR RHYTHM	The use of records of previous menstrual cycles to calculate the most fertile period of a woman's current menstrual cycle.
CASTRATION	The removal of the testes in the male or of the ovaries in the female.
CELL	The fundamental, microscopic unit of living substance, which alone or with other cells performs the body's basic functions.
CERVIX	The narrow opening at the neck of the uterus.
CHROMOSOMES	The material contained in the nucleus of the cell, which determines the heredity-related characteristics of the child.
CILIA	Tiny hairlike projections capable of lashing movement, as those, for instance, found in

	the lining of the inside walls of the vas deferens and the fallopian tubes.
CIRCUMCISION	The removal of all or part of the foreskin of the penis.
CLEAVAGE	The cell division immediately following fertilization.
CLIMAX	See ORGASM.
CLITORIS	The pea-shaped organ in the female located just above the urethra. The clitoris has many sensitive nerve tissues and plays a major part in female orgasm. It is often considered to be the female counterpart of the male penis.
COITUS	See SEXUAL INTERCOURSE.
COITUS INTERRUPTUS	Also known as "withdrawal"; sexual intercourse in which the penis is withdrawn from the vagina before ejaculation.
CONCEPTION	The merging of the female sex cell (ovum) and the male sex cell (sperm) in the fallopian tube.
CONDOM	A sheath or cover for the penis, which can be worn during sexual intercourse to prevent pregnancy and the spread of venereal diseases.
CONTRACEPTIVE	A device or method designed to prevent conception.
COPULATION	See SEXUAL INTERCOURSE.
CORPUS LUTEUM	Also known as the "yellow body." The name for the ovarian follicle when it takes on a new function after ovulation. The corpus luteum produces both progesterone and estrogen.

COWPER'S GLANDS   Male glands, which secrete fluids along the urethra during sexual excitement.

DEMOGRAPHER   A person involved in the statistical study of population topics such as births, deaths, migration, and marriage patterns.

DIAPHRAGM   A soft rubber bowl-like device inserted through the vagina to cover the entrance to the uterus so that sperm cannot enter. The diaphragm is used with sperm-killing chemical preparations.

DOUCHE   The rinsing out of the vagina with a syringe-type device. Not a form of birth control.

DOWN'S SYNDROME   See MONGOLISM.

DUCTUS DEFERENS   See VAS DEFERENS.

DYSMENORRHEA   Painful menstruation.

DYSPAREUNIA   Difficult or painful intercourse.

ECTOPIC PREGNANCY   A serious medical condition in which a fertilized egg becomes implanted in the fallopian tube or somewhere else other than the uterus.

EJACULATION   The expulsion of semen from the male body.

EMBRYO   The developing baby during its first two months, after which it is called a fetus.

ENDOMETRIUM   The inner lining of the uterus, which goes through cyclical changes to prepare for the possibility of implantation. When implantation occurs, the endometrium provides nourishment and protection for the growing baby.

EPIDIDYMIS

The long, coiled tubes near the testes, where the sperm stay while they mature.

EPISIOTOMY

A small incision in the area between the vagina and the anus, often made before childbirth, to enlarge the opening through which the baby will pass.

ERECTION

The condition of the penis when it becomes erect and rigid.

ESTROGEN

A basic female hormone produced by the follicle in the ovary; responsible for development of the female's secondary sex characteristics, and for the growth and maintenance of the uterus, fallopian tubes, and vagina.

ESTROUS CYCLES

Heat cycles of most nonhuman mammals that ensure that intercourse and ovulation occur at or about the same time.

FALLOPIAN TUBES

The two tubes with fingerlike fringes that attract the egg when it has been released from the ovary and serve to transport it to the uterus.

FAMILY PLANNING

A system of rational control over childbearing designed to prevent the birth of unwanted babies, and to allow desired timing of the wanted children.

FECUNDITY

The ability to have children.

FERTILIZATION

See CONCEPTION.

FETAL DEATH

The expulsion of a fetus that shows no sign of life; a stillbirth; generally statistically reported only after the twentieth week of pregnancy.

FETUS

The name given the growing baby from the

end of the second month of pregnancy until birth.

FIMBRIA

The fingerlike fringes of the fallopian tubes, which serve to attract the egg into the tubes once ovulation has occurred.

FOAM (CONTRACEPTIVE)

A sperm-killing preparation, which can be placed in the vagina just before sexual intercourse to block the entrance to the uterus and to kill sperm on contact.

FOLLICLE (OVARIAN)

The structure in the ovary in which the egg cells grow.

FORESKIN

The piece of skin that lies over the tip of the penis. Usually the foreskin is removed in a process known as circumcision.

FRATERNAL TWINS

Twins resulting from the fertilization of two eggs. Fraternal twins may be of the same sex or the opposite sex and have a different genetic makeup.

FRIGIDITY

The inability of a woman to respond sexually.

FSH

Follicle-stimulating hormone, which is released by the pituitary gland and acts (in the female) directly on the ovary, causing an egg within the follicle to begin to grow, and (in the male) on the testes to stimulate spermatogenesis.

GENITALS

The reproductive organs of a man or a woman.

GESTATION

See PREGNANCY.

GLAND

An organ that produces a specific product or secretion.

GONAD

Specific sex gland such as an ovary or testis.

GONADOTROPIC	The adjective describing those hormones that serve to stimulate either the ovary or the testis.
GYNECOLOGIST	A doctor who specializes in the area of medicine that deals with diseases of women, particularly diseases of the reproductive system.
HCG	See HUMAN CHORIONIC GONADOTROPIC HORMONE.
HERNIA	An abnormal protrusion of an organ (or part of it) through structures normally containing it; for instance, an interstitial or scrotal hernia.
HORMONE	A substance produced by a special type of gland to control functions of other organs.
HUMAN CHORIONIC GONADOTROPIC HORMONE (HCG)	A hormone secreted by the placenta, which serves to maintain the corpus luteum. HCG's presence in the urine is a common sign of pregnancy.
HYALURONIDASE	An enzyme released by sperm to chemically break down the protective layer of the egg.
HYMEN	The thin membrane that may or may not cover the opening of the vagina of a virgin girl.
HYPOPHYSIS	See PITUITARY GLAND.
HYSTERECTOMY	An operation in which a woman's uterus is removed.
IDENTICAL TWINS	Twins that have developed from the same egg. Identical twins are always of the same sex and have the same genetic makeup.

IMPLANTATION	The imbedding of a fertilized egg in the tissues of the lining of the uterus.
IMPOTENCE	The inability of the man to participate in or enjoy sexual intercourse.
INFANT MORTALITY	Deaths during the first year of life.
INGUINAL CANAL	The canal in the groin through which the testes descend to the scrotum prior to birth.
INJECTABLE CONTRACEPTIVES	"Birth-control shots" designed to provide contraceptive protection for an extended period—perhaps a month, or three months; "time-released" hormone injections.
INSEMINATION	The introduction of male sex cells into the woman's body, either through sexual intercourse or artificial means.
INTRAUTERINE DEVICE	A small, flexible device placed in the uterus to prevent either implantation or conception.
ICSH (INTERSTITIAL CELL-STIMULATING HORMONE)	The master-gland hormone in the male, which stimulates production of testosterone by the testes; identical chemically to the luteinizing hormone (LH) in the female.
LABIA MAJORA	Two rounded folds of fat tissue that extend from the mons pubis downward throughout the area of the vulva.
LABIA MINORA	The "small lips"; two parallel folds of soft tissue that begin at the clitoris and end in the lower vulva area.
LACTATION	The secretion of milk by the mammary glands after birth.

LAPAROSCOPIC
STERILIZATION

Female sterilization using a laparoscope, a thin stainless-steel tube that can be inserted through the abdomen to facilitate the sealing of the fallopian tubes.

LIBIDO

The commonly used word to describe sex drive or desire.

LUTEINIZING
HORMONE

Known as LH, a hormone produced by the pituitary gland to stimulate the release of an egg from the follicle. LH also plays a role in the development and functioning of the corpus luteum, or yellow body. LH is identical chemically to the male hormone ICSH.

MAMMARY GLANDS

Glands within the breasts that are capable of secreting milk after childbirth.

MENARCHE

The first menstrual period.

MENOPAUSE

The cessation of menstruation.

MENSTRUATION

The shedding of the lining of the uterus (endometrium) in the event pregnancy has not occurred.

MINI-PILL

A contraceptive agent containing a synthetic form of progesterone, which serves to prevent conception by changing the nature of the cervical mucus to prevent sperm from entering the uterus.

MISCARRIAGE

A spontaneous expulsion of the growing baby before it can survive on its own.

MITTELSCHMERZ

A cramp-type pain in the abdomen observed by some women at or near the time of ovulation.

MONGOLISM

A congenital malformation in which the child has slanted eyes, a large tongue, and a broad, short skull. Such children are often imbeciles.

MONS PUBIS   Also known as mons veneris; firm, cushion-like pubic-hair-covered mound of fat directly over the pubic bones.

MORNING-AFTER PILL   A drug (usually synthetic estrogen in the form of diethylstilbestrol) used as an emergency measure to prevent implantation following unprotected mid-cycle intercourse.

NUCLEUS   The specialized portion of a cell that contains the hereditary or genetic materials.

OBSTETRICIAN   A doctor who specializes in the field of medicine covering the care of women during pregnancy, labor, and the period just after birth.

ORGANS   Any group of tissues that perform a specific function or functions.

ORGASM   The final phase of sexual excitement in both a man and a woman; also known as a climax.

OVARY   The egg- and hormone-producing sex glands (gonads) of the female.

OVIDUCTS   See FALLOPIAN TUBES.

OVULATION   The process whereby the egg is released from the ovary.

OVUM   The egg cell produced by the female sex gland, the ovary, about every month between puberty and menopause.

PENIS   The male organ for both sexual intercourse and urination.

pH

The commonly used measure of alkalinity and acidity. pH 7 is the neutral point. Above pH 7 alkalinity increases, below pH 7 acidity increases.

PHYSIOLOGY

The study of the function of the human organism.

PITUITARY GLAND

Also known as the hypophysis or "master gland"; small gland in base of brain, which secretes hormones that regulate many human systems.

PLACENTA

The organ on the wall of the mother's uterus that is connected to the growing baby by an umbilical cord. The placenta is the organ through which the growing baby receives nourishment and protection against many diseases.

PREGNANCY

The state of a woman from the time of conception until the delivery of the child.

PREMENSTRUAL
TENSION

A syndrome experienced by some women in the days before the menstrual flow. Characterized by irritability and/or depression.

PROGESTERONE

The hormone of pregnancy, produced by the follicle after ovulation; acts together with estrogen to coordinate and regulate the events of the menstrual cycle.

PROLIFERATIVE
PHASE

That portion of the menstrual cycle that follows the menstrual flow and precedes ovulation. The proliferative phase is characterized by increased levels of estrogen.

PROSTAGLANDIN

A substance within the male semen that appears to increase the muscular activity of the uterus.

PROSTATE GLAND

A gland in the male near the bladder and the urethra that secretes a special type of fluid that aids in the maintenance and movement of sperm.

PUBERTY

The changes that occur about the age of twelve or thirteen in a girl and about thirteen or fourteen in a boy and ultimately allow participation in the reproductive process.

PUBIC BONES

Two small bones that meet at the narrowest part of the pelvic girdle to form the pubis.

PUBIS

The area at which the two pelvic bones join. After puberty, the pubis is covered with hair.

RHYTHM METHOD

A form of family planning in which the couple avoid sexual intercourse during the period of the female cycle when conception is most likely to occur.

SAFE PERIOD

The days during a woman's cycle when she is least likely to become pregnant.

SCROTUM

The fleshy pouch that contains the male testes and related organs.

SECRETORY PHASE

That portion of the menstrual cycle that follows ovulation and ends with the first day of the menstrual flow. The secretory phase is characterized by increased secretion of progesterone until mid-phase.

SEMEN

The liquid that contains the male sex cells and a variety of other secretions from within the male's body.

SEMINAL EMISSION

The product of ejaculation, a thick milky fluid usually containing several million

	sperm, which is ejaculated by the male during orgasm.
SEMINAL VESICLES	The two small sacs, located near the base of a man's bladder, which secrete a special type of fluid that aids the sperm in mobility.
SEXUAL INTERCOURSE	Also known as coitus, or copulation; the insertion of the penis into the vagina.
SMEGMA	A thick, cheesy secretion, which may accumulate at the tip of the penis.
SPERM	The male sex cell.
SPERMATOCYTE	A cell that will grow into a mature sperm cell.
SPERMATOGENESIS	The process during which sperm are developed in the testes.
SPERMICIDAL	Adjective to describe those chemicals that kill sperm.
SPERM "RESERVOIR"	See AMPULLA.
STERILE	Not fertile; unable either to become pregnant or fertilize an egg.
STERILIZATION	A medical procedure that results in an individual's being incapable of playing a role in reproduction.
SYPHILIS	An infectious venereal disease characterized first by chancre formation at the point of contact, and later by skin infections and eventual deterioration of muscles and the nervous system.
SYSTEM	A group of organs that work together in some complex vital process.

TEMPERATURE RHYTHM	The use of a basal-body thermometer to follow variations in temperature during a month, in an effort to predict the time of ovulation.
TESTIS	The male sex gland, or gonad, which produces the sperm.
TESTOSTERONE	Male sex hormone produced by the testes which, among other things, controls maturation in the male and the functioning of his reproductive system.
TISSUE	A group of cells, often with a specific function, as nervous tissue, muscular tissue, or connective tissue.
TUBAL LIGATION	Female sterilization by cutting and tying her fallopian tubes.
UMBILICAL CORD	The cord that connects the fetus with the placenta.
URETHRA	The tube that carries urine from the bladder to the outside of the body. In the male, the urethra also serves to conduct sperm.
UTERINE TUBES	See FALLOPIAN TUBES.
UTERUS	Also known as the womb. Hollow, pear-shaped organ in center of the lower abdomen, where a growing baby can receive protection and nourishment.
VAGINA	The muscular tube that serves both as the female organ for sexual intercourse and the birth canal.
VAGINAL INTROITUS	The external opening of the vagina.
VAS DEFERENS	The duct that carries sperm from the testes to the ejaculatory duct.

VASECTOMY	Male sterilization by cutting and tying the vas deferens.
VIRGIN	An individual who has not had sexual intercourse.
WET DREAM	The discharge of semen without sexual intercourse, usually occurring during sleep; also referred to as a nocturnal emission.
WITHDRAWAL	See COITUS INTERRUPTUS.
WOMB	See UTERUS.
ZERO POPULATION GROWTH	A demographic situation in which births and deaths are equal and there is no net change in population from year to year.
ZONA PELLUCIDA	The outer membrane of the female egg cell, which serves in a protective capacity.
ZYGOTE	The name given the new cell formed by the joining of an egg and sperm.

REFERENCES AND SUGGESTIONS FOR FURTHER READING

Those references marked with an asterisk (*) may be of particular interest to you.

CHAPTERS 1–5

Bell, G. *et al.*, *Textbook of Physiology and Biochemistry*. London: Churchill Livingston, 1972.
*Boston Children's Medical Center, *Pregnancy, Birth and the Newborn Baby*. New York: Delacorte Press, 1972.
Bourne, G., *Pregnancy*. London: Cassell, 1972.
Brooks, S., *Integrated Basic Science*. St. Louis: C. V. Mosby, 1966.
*Brown, F. and R. T. Kempton, *Sex Questions and Answers*, second edition. New York: McGraw-Hill, 1970.
*Burt, J. and L. Brower, *Education for Sexuality*. Philadelphia: W. B. Saunders, 1970.
Cederqvist, L. L. and F. Fuchs, "Antenatal Sex Determination," *Clinical Obstetrics and Gynecology* 13:159, 1970.
*Colman, A. and L. Colman, *Pregnancy: The Psychological Experience*. New York: Herder and Herder, 1971.
Crough, J. E., *Functional Human Anatomy*. Philadelphia: Lea & Febiger, 1972.
*Davson, H. *A Textbook of General Physiology*. Baltimore: Williams and Wilkins, 1970.
*Demarest, R. J. and J. J. Sciarra, *Conception, Birth and Contraception: A Visual Presentation*. New York: McGraw-Hill, 1969.
Diamond, M. *Perspectives in Reproduction and Sexual Behavior*. Bloomington, Indiana: Indiana University Press, 1968.
Diasio, R. B. and R. H. Glass, "Effects of pH on the Migration of X and Y Sperm," *Fertility and Sterility* 22:303, 1971.
*Dienhart, C. M., *Basic Human Anatomy and Physiology*. Philadelphia: W. B. Saunders, 1973.
Eastman, N. and L. Hellman, *Williams Obstetrics*, thirteenth edition. New York: Appleton-Century Crofts, 1966.
Easton, D., *Mechanisms of Body Function*. Englewood Cliffs, New Jersey: Prentice-Hall, 1963.
Edwards, L. F. and G. R. Gaughran, *Concise Anatomy*. New York: McGraw-Hill, 1971.
*Etzioni, A., "Sex Control, Science and Society," *Science*, 161:1107, 1968.
Fielding, W. L., *Pregnancy: The Best State of the Union*. New York: Thomas Y. Crowell, 1971.
Guerrero, R., "Sex Ratio: A Statistical Association with Type and Time of Insemination in the Menstrual Cycle," *International Journal of Fertility* 15:221, 1970.

*Guyton, A. C., *Function of the Human Body*. Philadelphia: W. B. Saunders, 1969.

Hafez, E. S. and T. N. Evans, *Human Reproduction*. New York: Harper & Row, 1973.

*Jacob, S. W. and C. A. Francone, *Structure and Function in Man*. Philadelphia: W. B. Saunders, 1965.

James, W., "Cycle Day of Insemination, Coital Rate and Sex Ratio," *Lancet*, January 16, 1971, p. 112.

Kahn, H. and A. Wiener, "The Next Thirty Years: A Framework for Speculation," in "Towards the Year 2000: Work in Progress," *Daedalus*, Summer 1967.

King, B. G. and M. J. Showers, *Human Anatomy and Physiology*. Philadelphia: W. B. Saunders, 1969.

Lippold, O. and F. Winton, *Human Physiology*. Boston: Little, Brown, 1968.

Odell, W. D. and D. L. Moyer, *Physiology of Reproduction*. St. Louis: C. V. Mosby, 1971.

Page, E., *Human Reproduction*. Philadelphia: W. B. Saunders, 1972.

*Pohlman, E., *The Psychology of Birth Planning*. Cambridge, Massachusetts: Schenkman, 1969.

Romanes, D. J., *Cunningham's Textbook of Anatomy*. London: Oxford University Press, 1972.

Roper, N., *Man's Anatomy, Physiology and Health*. Edinburgh: E. & S. Livingstone, 1969.

Selkurt, E., *Physiology*. Boston: Little, Brown, 1971.

Shearman, R. P., *Human Reproductive Physiology*. Oxford, England: Blackwell Scientific Publications, 1972.

Simons, G. L., *A History of Sex*. London: New English Library, 1970.

————, *Sex and Superstition*. London: Abelard-Schuman, 1973.

Tuttle, W. and B. Schottelius, B. A., *Textbook of Physiology*. St. Louis: C. V. Mosby, 1969.

Villee, C., *Biology*. Philadelphia: W. B. Saunders, 1967.

Warwick, R. and P. L. Williams, ed., *Anatomy*. Philadelphia: W. B. Saunders, 1973.

Weir, W. C. and T. D. Downs, "The Optimal Time for Conception," *Fertility and Sterility* 19:64, 1968.

*Whelan, E. M. and M. C. Quadland, *Human Reproduction and Family Planning: A Programmed Text*. Palo Alto, California: Syntex Laboratories, 1973.

*Whelan, E. M., "Can You Control Your Baby's Sex?" *Modern Bride*, June/July 1974.

————, "How Much Do You Know About Sex?" *Cosmopolitan*, Fall 1974.

CHAPTER 6

*"Abortion Warning: Dilation May Add to Miscarriage Risk," *Family Planning Digest*, #1, 6, November 1972.

Bakker, C. and C. Dightman, "Psychological Factors in Fertility Control," *Fertility and Sterility* 15:559, 1964.

Berman, E., "The Once a Month Pill," *Journal of Reproductive Medicine* 5:196, 1970.

*Brant, H. and M. Brant, *Dictionary of Pregnancy, Childbirth and Contraception*. London: Mayflower, 1971.

*Calderone, M., *Manual of Family Planning and Contraceptive Practice*. Baltimore: Williams and Wilkins, 1970.

Corson, S. L. and R. J. Bolognese, "Voluntary Interruption of Pregnancy: Its Psychiatric and Contraceptive Correlates," *Journal of Reproductive Medicine* 8:151, 1972.

*Demarest, R. and J. Sciarra, *Conception, Birth and Contraception*. New York: McGraw-Hill, 1969.

Di Saia, P. *et al.*, "Continuous Tablet Therapy for Oral Contraception," *Obstetrics and Gynecology* 31:119, 1968.

*Duffy, B. J. and M. J. Wallace, *Biological and Medical Aspects of Contraception*. Notre Dame, Indiana: Notre Dame Press, 1969.

Glass, R. and N. Kase, *Woman's Choice*. New York: Basic Books, 1970.

Green, S., *The Curious History of Contraception*. London: Ebury Press, 1971.

Harkavy, O. and J. Maier, "Research in Contraception and Reproduction: A Status Report, 1971," *Family Planning Perspectives* 3:15, 1971.

Havemann, E., *Birth Control*. New York: Time-Life Books, 1967.

*Himes, N. E., *Medical History of Contraception*. New York: Gamut Press, 1963.

*Kistner, R. W., *The Pill*. New York: Dell, 1969.

*Lehfeldt, H., "Willful Exposure to Unwanted Pregnancy (WEUP)," *American Journal of Obstetrics and Gynecology* 78:661, 1959.

Modern Methods of Birth Control. Planned Parenthood–World Population. New York, 1972.

*Peel, J. and M. Potts, *Textbook of Contraceptive Practice*. Cambridge, England: University Press, 1969.

Rudell, H. *et al.*, *Birth Control*. New York: The Macmillan Company, 1973.

Tyler, E. T. *et al.*, "Present Status of Injectable Contraceptives: Results of Seven Years' Study," *Fertility and Sterility* 21:469, 1970.

Understanding. Raritan, New Jersey: Ortho Pharmaceutical Corporation, 1971.

*Whelan, E. and M. C. Quadland, *Human Reproduction and Family Planning: A Programmed Text*. Palo Alto, California: Syntex Laboratories, 1973.

CHAPTERS 7–9

American Medical Association, *Human Sexuality*. Chicago, 1972.

*Anthony, E. J. and T. Benedek, *Parenthood: Its Psychology and Psychopathology*, Boston: Little, Brown, 1970.

Arnstein, H. S., *Your Growing Child and Sex*. New York: Avon, 1968.

Ayd, F. J., Jr., "The Teenager and Contraception," *Pediatric Clinics of North America* 16:355, 1969.

Berman, L. H., "Freedom and Sexuality," *Diseases of the Nervous System* 30:784, 1969.

*Blanzaco, A. C., *VD: Facts You Should Know*. New York: Lothrop, Lee and Shepard, 1970.

Chesser, E., *Is Chastity Outmoded?* London: Heinemann, 1950.

*Colton, H., *Our Sexual Evolution*. New York: Franklin Watts, 1972.

Coombs, L. *et al.*, "Premarital Pregnancy and Status Before and After Marriage," *American Journal of Sociology* 75:800, 1970.

Coombs, L. and R. Freedman, "Premarital Pregnancy, Childspacing and Later Economic Achievement," *Population Studies* 24:389, 1970.

Crain, I. J., "Sex and Love," *Diseases of the Nervous System* 30:774, 1969.

Dalrymple, W., "A Doctor Speaks of College Students and Sex," *Journal of American College Health Association* 15:279, 1967.

Farnsworth, D., *Sexual Problems in College: Current Psychiatric Therapies*. New York: Grune & Stratton, 1966.

Freud, S., *Outline of Psychoanalysis*. New York: W. W. Norton, 1949.

Friedman, J., "Conscience and Its Relation to Sex," *New York State Medical Journal* 70:2323, 1970.

Fromm, E., *The Art of Loving*. New York: Bantam Books, 1963.

Gadpaille, W. J., "Adolescent Sexuality and the Struggle Over Authority," *Journal of School Health* 40:479, 1970.

Gerstle, M. L., "Prevalent Sexual Misconceptions," *American Journal of Psychiatry* 130:1403, 1973.

Goldman, G. D. and D. S. Milman, *Modern Woman: Her Psychology and Sexuality*. Springfield: Charles C Thomas, 1969.

Grold, L. J., "Swinging: Sexual Freedom or Neurotic Escapism?" *American Journal of Psychiatry* 27:163, 1970.

Halleck, S., "Sex and Mental Health on the Campus," *Journal of the American Medical Association* 200:684, 1967.

Harding, F., "The Adolescent on Campus," *Woman Physician* 25:88, 1970.

Hempel, W. V., "Sexual Freedom: A Reaction Formation?" *American Journal of Psychiatry* 130:722, 1973.

*Hern, M., "Is Pregnancy Really Normal?" *Family Planning Perspectives* 3:5, 1971.

*Hettlinger, R., "A Father Speaks Out on Sex," *Parents' Magazine*, June 1967.

Hunter, T. A., "Sex and Its Problems," *The Practitioner* 198:453, 1967.

James, J., "Sexual Activity and Cancer," *Lancet*, April 11, 1970, p. 776.

*"Johnny Gets the Word," *New York City Health Department*, 1968.

Josselyn, I. M., *Adolescence*. New York: Harper & Row, 1971.

Kaufman, S., "Adolescence and Human Sexuality," *Diseases of the Nervous System* 30:777, 1969.

Kilander, H. F., *Sex Education in the Schools*. New York: Macmillan, 1970.

*Lamers, W., "Problems of Teenagers Presented to Obstetricians and Gynecologists," *Clinical Obstetrics and Gynecology* 13:727, 1970.

*Lee, R. V., "The Importance of Virginity in 1972," *Yale Journal of Biology and Medicine* 45:iii, 1972.

———, "What About the Right to Say 'No'?" *New York Times Magazine*, September 16, 1973.

*Levin, M., "The Teenager and the Sexual Revolution," *Southwestern Medicine* 48:104, 1967.

———, "Healthy Sexual Behavior," *Pediatric Clinics of North America* 16:329, 1969.

Lief, H., "Sex and the Medical Educator," *Journal of the American Medical Woman's Association* 23:195, 1968.

Lobl, M. *et al.*, "Maternal Age and Intellectual Functioning of Offspring," *Johns Hopkins Medical Journal* 128:347, 1971.

Malinowski, B., *Parenthood: The Basis of Social Structure*. New York, Macaulay, 1930.

Masterson, J. F., "The Implication of the Sexual Revolution in the Adolescent's Search for Sexual Identity," *Maryland State Medical Journal* 18:53, 1969.

May, R., "Anecdotes for the New Puritanism," *Saturday Review* 49:19, 1966.

McCranie, M., "Misuse of Sex by the Adolescent Girl," *Journal of the Medical Association of Georgia* 57:159, 1968.

*Menken, J., "The Health and Social Consequences of Teenage Childbearing," *Family Planning Perspectives* 4:45, 1972.

Miller, I., "The Don Juan Character," *Human Sexuality*, April 1969.

Moghissi, K. *et al.*, "Epidemiology of Cervical Cancer," *American Journal of Obstetrics and Gynecology* 100:607, 1968.

Munroe, R. L. and Munroe, R. H., "Male Pregnancy Symptoms and Cross Cultural Identity in Three Societies," *Journal of Social Psychology* 84:11, 1971.

Morton, R. S., *Sexual Freedom and Venereal Disease*. London: Peter Owen, 1971.

Oberst, B., "Unlock the Door on Youth Problems: The Adolescent from Eleven to Sixteen Years," *Nebraska State Medical Journal* 56:343, 1971.

Osofsky, H. J., "Adolescent Sexual Behavior: Current Status and Anticipated Trends for the Future," *Clinical Obstetrics and Gynecology* 14:393, 1971.

*Pohlman, E., *Psychology of Birth Planning*. Cambridge, Massachusetts: Schenkman, 1969.

————, "The Timing of the First Birth: A Review of Effects," *Eugenics Quarterly* 15:252, 1968.

Population and the American Future, The Report of the Commission on Population Growth and the American Future. New York: Signet, 1972.

Powers, G. P. and W. Baskin, *Sex Education: Issues and Directives*. New York: Philosophical Library, 1969.

Reiss, Ira, "Social Class and Premarital Sexual Permissiveness: A Reexamination," *American Sociological Review* 30:747, 1965.

*Richardson, S. and A. F. Guttmacher, *Childbearing: Its Social and Psychological Aspects*. Baltimore: Williams and Wilkins, 1967.

*Rosebury, T., *Microbes and Morals: The Strange Story of Venereal Disease*. New York: Viking Press, 1971.

Rubin, I. and L. A. Kirkendall, eds., *Sex in the Adolescent Years: New Directions in Guiding and Teaching Youth*. New York: Association Press, 1968.

"Sexual Promiscuity Among Students," *British Medical Journal* (editorial), March 25, 1967, p. 711.

Shainess, N., "The Problem of Sex Today," *American Journal of Psychiatry* 124:94, 1968.

*Shapiro, S. *et al.*, *Infant, Perinatal, Maternal and Childhood Mortality in the United States*. Cambridge: Harvard University Press, 1968.

*Sherman, J. A., *On the Psychology of Women*. Springfield: Charles C Thomas, 1971.

Sorensen, R., *Adolescent Sexuality in Contemporary America*. New York: World Publishing, 1973.

Spicer, F., "Sexual Problems in Adolescence," *Proceedings of the Royal Society of Medicine* 61:510, 1968.

Stamler, J. *et al.*, "Epidemiology of Cancer of the Cervix," *American Journal of Public Health* 57:791, 1967.

Szasz, G., "Adolescent Sexual Activity," *The Canadian Nurse* 67:39, October 1971.

Walters, P. A., "Promiscuity in Adolescence," *American Journal of Orthopsychiatry* 35:670, 1965.

Weintraub, W., "Adolescence," *The Practice of Medicine*, volume 10, 1972.

Whelan, E. M., "American Population Policy: Which Way from Here?" *Connecticut College Alumnae Quarterly*, Summer 1970.

———, "Estimates of the Ultimate Family States of Children Born Out-of-Wedlock in Massachusetts," *Journal of Marriage and the Family*, November 1972.

———, "The Temporal Relationship of Marriage, Conception and Birth," *Demography* 9:399, 1972.

———, "Illegitimate and Premaritally Conceived Births in Massachusetts," *Social Biology* 19:9, 1972.

———, *Teenage Childbearing: Extent and Consequences*, Consortium on Early Childbearing and Childrearing, January 1973.

———, "Parenthood: If 'Yes,' When?" *Bride Magazine*, August/September 1974.

———, "How Much Does It Cost to Have a Baby?" *Glamour*, November 1974.

Wigfield, A., "Attitudes Toward Venereal Disease in a Permissive Society," *British Medical Journal*, November 6, 1971, p. 342.

Wolfish, M., "Adolescent Sexuality," *The Practitioner* 210:226, 1973.

Zelnick, M. and J. Kantner, "Sexuality, Contraception and Pregnancy Among Young Unwed Females in the United States," *Final Report to the Commission on Population Growth and the American Future*. Washington: Government Printing Office, 1973.

Index

Abortion, 95–97, 110–112
Afterbirth, 66
Ampulla. *See* Sperm "reservoir"
Androgens, 14, 98
Anus, 30
Areola, 31
Arousal, sexual, 108, 133–134
Artificial insemination, 50
Aspirator abortion, 97

Baby
   birth of, 66–67
   illegitimate, 110–111
   pregnancy, 58–66
Bag of waters, 62, 66
Bartholin's glands, 30
Basal-body-temperature rhythm. *See* rhythm method
Behavior, sexual, 105–137
   parents and, 107
   personal standards, 132–133, 136–137
   promiscuity, 105–108, 132
   stimulation and arousal, 108, 133–134
   tradition and revolution in, 103–106
   See also premarital sex; sex; sexual intercourse

Birth. *See* baby; conception; pregnancy
Birth control, 72–99
   abortion, 95–97, 110–112
   current methods of, 75–99
   early methods of, 73–74
   and family planning, 70, 107 145–146
   future of, 97–99
   motivation for, 99
   side effects of, 78, 91
   and V.D., 82
Birth-control shot, 79, 92
Bladder, 8, 9, 10, 20
Breasts
   anatomy and physiology of, 31–32
   breast feeding, 31, 67
   mammary glands in, 31, 66, 67
   pregnancy and, 63, 66, 67
Bulbo-urethal glands. *See* Cowper's glands

Calendar rhythm. *See* rhythm method
Cancer
   of cervix, 11, 118
   of penis, 11
   of vagina, 95

Careers, family planning and, 141–142
Castration, 84
Cervix
  anatomy and physiology of, 29, 50,
    51, 62, 69, 77, 89, 91, 92, 95,
    96, 117
  cancer of, 11, 118
Chancre, *See* syphilis
Chromosomes, 16, 44
  and gender, 3, 17, 26, 52
Cilia, 8, 28
Circumcision, 10, 11
Cleavage, 58
Clitoris, 30, 31, 69
Coil. *See* intrauterine device
Coitus. *See* sexual intercourse
Coitus interruptus, 81, 82, 92
Conception, 44, 62, 70, 81
  prevention of, 72–99
  See also fertilization
Condom, 75, 82, 83, 85, 90, 118
Congenital syphilis, 117
Contraception/contraceptives, 72–99,
  107, 145. *See also* birth control
Corpus luteum, 39, 40, 59
Cowper's glands, 8
Culdoscopy. *See* sterilization, female

Diaphragm, 75, 89–90, 92, 97
Diethylstilbestrol (DES). *See* morning-
  after pill
Dilation and curettage (D & C), 95, 96
Divorce, 111, 143, 147
Douche, 94
Dysmenorrhea, 36

Ectopic pregnancy, 69
Egg cell
  fertilization of, 3, 40, 50, 51, 52,
    54–55, 58–59
  growth of, 37
  and LH, 39
  and ovulation, 34–35, 43, 46, 48, 49,
    54, 75, 79
  physiology of, 44–45, 46, 68
  production of, 28
Ejaculation, 7, 8, 9, 19, 20, 21–23, 44,
  49–51, 68, 81, 129
Ejaculatory duct, 6, 8, 84
Embryo, 58, 60, 61, 62
Endometrium, 29, 30, 36, 58–59, 69
Epididymis, 6, 7, 8, 19, 66, 84
Erection, 19, 20, 21, 23, 49, 83, 102
Estrogen
  in birth-control pill, 76–77, 91, 94
  role in menstrual cycle, 37–40, 76–77

Estrogen:
  secretion and function of, 32, 59, 69
Estrous cycle, 102

Fallopian tubes
  anatomy and physiology of, 28, 29, 39,
    43, 69, 75, 77, 80, 116
  and fertilization, 45, 49, 50, 51, 52,
    58, 68, 69, 75
Family planning, 70, 72, 75, 80, 83,
  106–107, 145, 148. *See also* birth
  control; population growth; zero
  population growth
Fertile period, 48
Fertility, 148
Fertility drugs, 55–56
Fertilization, 52, 54, 55, 58–59. *See also*
  conception; egg; fallopian tubes; sperm
Fetus, 60, 61, 62, 63
Foam, vaginal, 90
Follicle, 16, 37, 38, 59
Follicle-stimulating hormone (FSH), 14,
  16, 17, 32, 36, 37, 76–77
Foreplay, 69. *See also* sexual intercourse
Foreskin, 10
Fraternal twinning, 55
French letter, 82. *See also* condom

Genitals. *See* penis; vagina
Glans, 10
Gonorrhea, 113, 115–116

Hernia, 4
Homosexuality, 123, 134–136
Hormones
  androgen, 14, 98
  estrogen, 32, 37–40, 59, 69, 76-77,
    91, 94, 97
  FSH 14, 16, 17, 32, 36, 37, 76–77
  HCG, 59
  LH, 38, 39, 40, 59, 77
  and menstrual cycle, 87, 88
  pituitary, 11, 12, 14, 32, 36, 37, 38,
    66, 76, 77
  progesterone, 39, 40, 59, 66, 69, 76,
    77, 88, 91
  testosterone, 14, 32, 98
Human chorionic gonadotropic hormone
  (HCG), 59
Hyaluronidase, 51, 52
Hymen, 30

Identical twinning, 55
Implantation, 58, 69
Infanticide, 73, 95
Infertility, 72

Inguinal canal, 3, 4
Interstitial cell, 14
Interstitial cell-stimulating hormone
(ICSH), 14, 32, 38
Intrauterine device (IUD), 75, 92–93, 94,
97
Intravaginal ring, 97

Kissing, 133

Labia majora, 31
Labia minora, 31
Labor, 66
Lactation, 67
Laparoscopic sterilization. *See*
sterilization, female
Lesbianism, 134
Loop. *See* intrauterine device
Luteinizing hormone (LH), 38, 39, 40
59, 77

Mammary gland(s), 31, 66, 67. *See also*
breasts
Marriage, 131
teenage, 143, 144
and divorce, 143
and parenthood, 144–145
Master gland. *See* pituitary gland
Masturbation, 22, 23, 69, 129
Menstrual cycle, 33–40, 45, 46, 47, 48
54, 57, 59
Menstruation, 26, 33–40, 76, 79, 80,
85–88, 91, 94, 102
Mini-pill, 75, 91, 92
Miscarriage, 70
Mittelschmerz, 46
Mongolism, 148
Mons pubis, 30
Morning-after pill, 94, 95
Morning sickness, 67
Multiple birth, 55

Nipple, 31
Nocturnal emission, 21, 22, 23

Once-a-month pill, 97
Oral contraceptives, 75–76, 79–80,
92, 97
Orgasm
female, 31, 68–69, 108
male, 21, 49, 69, 81, 82, 84, 108
Out-of-wedlock births, 99, 109, 110-112,
113, 126
Ovaries
anatomy and physiology of, 26

Ovaries:
and hormonal secretion, 32, 37, 38, 77
and egg production, 37, 43, 53, 54,
55, 75, 80
Oviducts. *See* fallopian tubes
Ovulation
definition of, 34
effect of body, 51
and menstruation, 35, 46, 47, 48, 87,
88
and mini-pill, 91
occurrence of, 46, 47, 48, 51, 87, 88
prevention of, 77–80, 98
and sterilization, 80
Parenthood, 99, 144–145, 147
Penis
anatomy and physiology of, 6, 9–10,
19–23, 30–31
circumcision of, 10–11
erection of, 19–23
and ejaculation, 20–23, 51, 81, 82
function of, 9–10
size of, 32
and sexual intercourse, 23, 69, 81
Petting, 133–134
Pill, The, 76–79, 80, 90, 92, 93, 97,
107, 109, 112–113, 125
Pituitary gland
and hormone secretion, 12, 14, 32, 66
76–77
location of, 11
role in menstrual cycle, 36–38
Placenta, 61, 62, 66
Population growth, 54, 70, 72–75, 106–107,
145–147. *See also* birth control;
zero population growth
Pregnancy
complications in, 69–70, 148
and conception, 40, 46–48, 51
description of, 59–70
effect on uterus, 29
fertile period, 46–48
and male, 3, 67
myth about, 53, 72–74, 109
unwanted, 99, 109–113, 126
Premarital sex, 102–149. *See also*
behavior, sexual; sex; sexual intercourse
Primary spermatocytes, 16, 17
Progesterone, 39, 40, 59, 66, 69, 76,
77, 88, 91
Promiscuity, 122–123, 132
Prostaglandin, 51
Prostate gland, 6, 9, 20, 84
Puberty, 18

Quickening. *See* pregnancy

Reproductive system, 2–11. *See also* names of specific glands and organs
Reversible vasectomy, 98
Rhythm method, 75, 85–88, 92
Rubber, 82. *See also* condom

Saline induction. *See* abortion
Scrotum, 3, 4, 6, 10, 18, 26
Secondary spermatocytes, 17
Semen, 21, 49, 51, 68, 73, 74, 81, 82, 84
Seminal emissions, 21, 22, 23, 35, 36, 102, 129
Seminal vesicles, 6, 7, 11, 20, 84
Sex
    attitudes toward, 103–107
    determination of, 53, 54, 58, 62
    emotional aspect of, 122–137, 141–142
    moral standards and, 133–134
    myths about, 42, 43
    physical maturity and, 102–113, 119, 122, 124–125
    and unwanted pregnancy, 99, 109–113, 126, 137, 149
    and venereal disease, 113–118, 126
    See also behavior, sexual; premarital sex; sexual intercourse
Sexual intercourse
    attitudes toward, 102–106
    and condom, 82
    consequences of, 23, 102–106
    and menstrual cycle, 48–54, 60, 86–87
    and morning-after pill, 94
    myths about, 122–137
    and orgasm, 69
    and parenthood, 99
    and pregnancy, 45, 48–49, 50, 72–74
    premarital, 102–149
    and spermicides, 90–91
Sheath, 82. *See also* condom
Smegma, 11
Sperm
    and birth control, 75, 82, 92, 94
    ejaculation of, 7, 8, 9, 19, 20, 21 23, 29, 49–51, 68, 81
    and fertilization, 23, 28, 30, 52, 53, 58–59, 68, 84, 85, 88, 90
    production of, 4, 6, 14, 16, 17, 18
    structure of, 28, 44, 45, 49, 50, 51
    theories about, 73–74
    and V.D., 116
Spermatogenesis, 16, 17, 18, 98. *See also* sperm, production of
Spermatogonium, 16

Spermicides, 75, 92, 89–91
Sperm "reservoir," 6, 8, 19, 20, 21, 84
Spiral. *See* intrauterine device
Sterility, 69
Sterilization
    female, 75, 79, 80, 81, 92
    male, 83, 84, 85
Subdermal implants, 97
Syphilis, 113, 114–115, 116–117, 126

Testes, 3, 4, 6, 7, 12, 14, 16, 17, 18, 19, 21, 26, 28, 53, 84
Testosterone, 14, 32, 98
Treponema pallidum. See syphillis
Tubal ligation. *See* sterilization, female
Twins, 54–55

Umbilical cord, 61, 66
Urethra, 6, 8, 9, 20, 21, 51, 69, 81 84
Urine test, for pregnancy, 59
Uterus
    anatomy and physiology of, 28–30, 50
    and birth control, 75, 79, 80, 89–95
    and fertilization, 50, 52, 58
    and menstruation, 33, 37, 39–40
    and pregnancy, 30, 35–40, 60–69

Vagina
    anatomy and physiology of, 29, 30, 33, 62, 95
    and birth control, 75, 77, 80, 81, 82, 85, 88, 90, 92, 95, 97
    cancer of, 95
    and menstruation, 33, 40
    and sexual intercourse, 50, 51, 54, 68, 69
    and V.D., 111
Vas deferens, 6, 8, 9, 19, 28, 29, 39, 84, 98
Vasectomy, 75, 83, 84, 85, 92, 98
Venereal disease (V.D.), 113–118, 126
Virginity, 123–124
Voice change, 14

Wasserman test, 118
Wet dream. *See* nocturnal emission
Withdrawal, 75, 81, 82, 85
Womb. *See* uterus

Yellow body. *See* corpus luteum

Zero population growth, 72, 145
Zona pellucida, 44